CATALYST CODE

CATALYST CODE

The Strategies Behind the
World's Most Dynamic Companies

David S. Evans and Richard Schmalensee

Harvard Business School Press
Boston, Massachusetts

Library of Congress Cataloging-in-Publication Data
 Evans, David S. (David Sparks), 1954-
  Catalyst code : the strategies behind the worlds most dynamic companies / David S. Evans and Richard Schmalensee.
     p. cm.
  ISBN 978-1-4221-0199-5 (hardcover : alk. paper) 1. Multi-sided platform businesses. 2. Strategic alliances (Business) I. Schmalensee, Richard. II. Title.
  HD9999.M78E94 2007
  658'.046—dc22

                                                                    2006034707

The paper used in this publication meets the requirements of the American National Standard for Permanence of Paper for Publications and Documents in Libraries and Archives Z39.48-1992.

With love and thanks
to our wives for their love
and support

Contents

Acknowledgments

This book is the result of a journey that we began around 2000. We are deeply thankful to those who helped us embark on this expedition as well as the many who have helped us along the way. The journey began with discussions with our colleagues Jean-Charles Rochet and Jean Tirole at the University of Toulouse in France. They had the deep insight about "two-sided businesses" that you will learn more about in the following pages. We benefited enormously from early drafts of their theoretical work on this topic. Importantly, they discovered that these two-sided businesses do not follow many of the traditional laws of economics. Around the same time, we began researching and collecting data on the important new genus of business models that they had identified. Our research has been continually enriched through discussions with our Toulousian friends.

We decided in late 2004 to embark on a long-term research project to understand what made these so-called two-sided businesses tick and to plan a book about our findings. To complement the emerging theoretical literature, we wanted to study a large number of businesses throughout the global economy from secondary sources and also to learn about some of them in depth through personal interviews with key players. We turned to Market Platform Dynamics (MPD), a consulting firm with which we are both affiliated, to conduct much of the basic research work.

The effort was led by Karen L. Webster, MPD's president. The key team members at MPD were Kirstyn Walton and Terry Xie. They were assisted at various points by Melissa DiBella and Laura Gee from LECG, LLC. We are extraordinarily grateful to this team for the hard work and diligence they put into this effort. Karen, in particular, improved in numerous ways the book we planned to write and contributed significantly to the substance and style of the following pages.

It would be impossible to overstate the benefits we obtained from our interviews with numerous people in business. All of these were conducted off the record, and we seldom cite specific conversations in the course of the book. But many men and women helped deepen our understanding through their gracious willingness to spend time with us. (Almost all interviews were conducted by the authors personally.) We list the people we talked to, alphabetically and without company affiliations: J. Allard, Raj Amin, Brian Arbogast, David Aronchick, Tim Attinger, Robbie Bach, Cathy Baron-Tamraz, Michael Bowling, Gerald Cavanagh, Alan Citron, Dallas Clement, Michael Clinton, David Cole, Christa Davies, Michael Dearing, Suzanne DelBene, Chris Donlay, Charles Fitzgerald, David Frear, Brian Gallagher, Robert Goldberg, Claude Green, Alan Harper, Scott Hatfield, James Healy, Carl Atsushi Hirano, Nanako Kato, Randy Komisar, Larry Kramer, Mitchell Kurtzman, Ed Lichty, Steve Lifflick, David Nagel, Takeshi Natsuno, Martha Nelson, Craig Neumark, Ray Ozzie, David Payne, Will Poole, Paul Scanlan, Warren Schlichting, Amy Stevenson, Sally Sussman, Dwight Witherspoon, and David Zaslav. We are particularly grateful for these frank conversations because, even more than providing factual information, they helped shape and test our thinking about the strategic issues discussed in this volume. We wish we could have shared with the reader all the insights we obtained from talking to these extraordinary individuals.

We have collaborated on some of the research discussed in this book with Professor Andrei Hagiu of Harvard Business School and MPD. Andrei is also affiliated with Market Platform Dynamics and was our coauthor on *Invisible Engines: How Software Platforms Drive Innovation and Transform Industries* (Cambridge, MA: MIT Press, 2006). That book reported our work on software platforms, which we also discuss somewhat in this book. We have also worked closely over many years with Howard Chang of LECG, LLC, on the payment card industry. We have gleaned many insights on that industry from Howard and have relied on research he has conducted or supervised over the years. Our friends and colleagues have been wonderful sources of support and inspiration for this work. They don't necessarily agree with us about anything, which is part of the joy of working with them. Only we, of course, bear any responsibility for whatever defects the ultimate result may have.

1

What Is a Catalyst?

Dig the well before you are thirsty.

—Chinese proverb

One day in 1949, Frank McNamara was having lunch in Manhattan. Halfway through his coffee, he realized he had forgotten his wallet and checkbook. Cash and check were the only ways to pay back then. While he was waiting for his wife to come to his rescue, he devised a scheme for a card that consumers could present to merchants for payment. Only half of his idea was new. Until then, many department stores and other merchants had given metal "charga plates" to their better customers, who could present this identification and pay their charges later. But many merchants, particularly restaurants, didn't offer this sort of credit, and people typically had to sign up for a separate account at each merchant that did. McNamara's innovation was to create a single card that many merchants would take for payment.

After his lunch faux pas, McNamara started Diners Club. His new company gave cards—then made of cardboard—to several hundred well-off residents of Manhattan. Those lucky recipients didn't have to pay anything and were told they would get a monthly bill for their charges. Diners Club got restaurants—fourteen at first—to accept the cards for payment and pay this new card company 7 percent of the meal tab in exchange. His scheme worked: cardholders started charging meals at restaurants, and restaurants appreciated the convenience and added patronage.

A year after Diners Club's launch, McNamara had signed up 330 restaurants, hotels, and nightclubs, along with 42,000 cardholders.[1] By then, cardholders had to pay a $5 annual fee that just about equaled the value of the free float they got from having to pay their bill only once a month. Diners Club made most of its profit from the merchants, which were still taking a 7 percent haircut. This "club" grew rapidly as more cardholders attracted more merchants and more merchants drew more cardholders. By 1956, almost $54 million of transactions ($315 million in 2005 dollars) were taking place on these cards at merchants from Boston to Anchorage to Tahiti.[2]

Diners Club had a good run during the 1950s but lost ground as its success attracted even more creative entrants, such as American Express. McNamara's epiphany about a card that would facilitate transactions between merchants and consumers led, however, to a massive global industry that provides the most widely accepted currency worldwide and has generated enormous profits for many of its participants. Fifty-five years after he forgot his checkbook, U.S. consumers charged $2.5 trillion at 4.9 million merchants using one of their 960 million credit or debit cards. American banks alone earned profits of $33 billion just from issuing credit cards.[3]

The Catalyst and Its Agents

Like many great innovators, Diners Club recognized that there was an enormous untapped source of value in the marketplace. Merchants and consumers wanted to transact with each other more easily, but they couldn't do it on their own. Each would benefit if someone got them together. McNamara did just that by persuading merchants and consumers to become members of the same community. This new club facilitated merchants and consumers doing business with each other. The card was the key to the club.

Diners Club was an *economic catalyst* (see the box "Economic Catalysts"). It wasn't the first and won't be the last. Microsoft's Windows operating system might be the most ubiquitous and well known economic catalyst of our era. In 2004, companies that sold applications that ran on Windows had worldwide revenues of $42 billion.[4] Yet Microsoft didn't charge them for using the company's crown jewels to power their applications, even though Microsoft had spent billions writing and debugging Windows. Computer manufacturers selling machines for homes or small offices paid an average of $92 per copy for licensing Windows to install on their machines.[5] That's far less than many application programs cost. This carefully designed business and pricing model is typical of catalysts. It helped make Bill Gates the richest man in the world.

Today, if you go through the *Forbes* list of the world's richest people, you will find many others who have made their fortunes by developing or shepherding catalysts. Some—like Pierre Omidyar, the inventor of eBay; or Larry Page and Sergey Brin, the founders of Google—became wealthy by tapping into the power of the Internet revolution to create valuable catalysts. But many catalysts

---

Economic Catalysts

Economic catalyst. An entity that has (a) two or more groups of customers; (b) who need each other in some way; but (c) who can't capture the value from their mutual attraction on their own; and (d) rely on the catalyst to facilitate value-creating reactions between them. For-profit businesses, joint ventures, cooperatives, standard-setting bodies, and governments operate catalysts.

Catalytic reaction. In the economy, the process by which value is created by facilitating the interaction between two or more mutually interdependent groups of customers.

are firmly rooted in the old economy. Alfred Taubman made a fortune from shopping malls, another catalyst that brings together two groups of customers: shoppers and shopkeepers. Others, such as Silvio Berlusconi, Rupert Murdoch, and Kenneth Thomson, made their fortunes from advertising-supported television and newspapers—both catalysts that attract one set of customers (readers) by offering interesting content while selling their eyeballs to another set of customers (advertisers).

How does a catalyst work? In chemistry, a catalyst is a substance that causes or accelerates a reaction between two (or more) other agents. The reaction typically creates a substance that is more valuable than the agents that created it. Yet the catalyst doesn't disappear. It can, therefore, create great value at little cost.

In business, a catalyst causes or accelerates reactions between two or more customer groups. These customer groups are attracted to each other. They need each other in some way. But without the catalyst, the two groups might never come together. The innovation that the successful catalyst introduces is essentially a way to make it easier for the two groups to come together and interact with one another. Catalysts can't force their customer groups to interact. Instead, they create convenient and appealing platforms that attract and benefit both sides. In the case of Diners Club, both restaurants and diners recognized the advantages of the catalytic power of the payment card. And, as in chemistry, the power of the catalyst in business remains even after it has brought two different groups together. It can continue to create significant value at relatively little additional cost.

The Catalyst Boom

Once you recognize what a catalyst is, you will see that catalysts play a growing role in many industries. Much as with the pattern recognition puzzles that psychologists sometimes use, it is hard to discern a catalyst until you know what to look for. You will discover that auction houses, financial exchanges, and nightclubs are catalysts. So are the Palm operating system, the Sony PlayStation, TiVo, and i-mode, the most popular wireless Internet service in Japan.

Although some catalysts are as old as business itself, in the years ahead we are likely to see catalysts play an increasingly prominent role in the economy. Indeed, a significant portion of the value created by today's economy now comes from catalysts and their communities. This development is a result of three related technological developments in the last quarter century.

The first is the dramatic reduction in the cost of computer processing and storage. These unprecedented price drops have made it cheaper and more efficient to operate platforms such as the Visa card network and auto auctions run by Manheim, the largest auto auction company in the world.

The second important technological development has been the dramatic reduction in communication costs and the rapid spread of broadband connections. These developments have made it easier for groups of people to interact with one another, regardless of location. As a result, people can easily conduct commerce over vast distances or arrange virtual meeting places to talk, exchange information, or create communities. Catalysts such as eBay have leveraged this.

The third development, and perhaps the least well known, is the rise of software platform technologies. Yet software platforms not only serve as catalysts to bring different groups of people together, they are increasingly the engines running many businesses.[6] When we think of TiVo and Xbox, for example, we tend to focus on their tangible aspects—the hardware that we plug in and turn on. But software is at the heart of these and many other products. The catalytic power of these software platforms is what transforms them from merely interesting ideas to powerful businesses that can reshape existing industries and build new ones.

Among other things, these new developments make it easier to solve the classic chicken-and-egg problem that bedevils new catalysts. To make the Diners Club card successful, Frank McNamara needed to persuade restaurants that there would be a sufficient number of potential customers wanting to use the card. At the same time, he had to convince diners that there was a critical mass of restaurants willing to accept the card. How do you get both sides to come on board at once? A successfully catalyst must find a way to win over both sides of the market more or less at once.

Creating Value Through Catalytic Reactions

Getting the formula right for a successful catalyst is harder than for an ordinary business, and most catalysts fail. And even though the payment card industry has had a profound impact on everyday life and produced plenty of profit for its participants, it hasn't generated the gargantuan paydays some catalyst entrepreneurs have seen. Setting off and managing a catalytic reaction among economic agents requires ingenuity, stamina, and a sound business strategy executed with steadiness and agility.

McNamara found that the 7/0 solution—7 percent from the merchants and essentially nothing from the cardholders—started and sustained the Diners Club reaction. How he arrived at this is lost to history. But if he hadn't hit on this golden pair, he might have gotten too few merchants to entice cardholders or too few cardholders to attract merchants. Or he might have found another solution that brought both groups en masse into his club but didn't leave him with enough profit to grow his system.

Bleeding cash, American Express was ready to exit the card business in 1961, three years after it had entered with a splash. But then it tried a dramatic shift in strategy: it raised its prices to cardholders by lifting the annual fee from $6 to $8.[7] That was just enough to make the American Express card profitable without driving away cardholders. The catalytic reaction was sustained. Building on this nimble move, American Express went on to dominate the card business for more than twenty years. Its less agile predecessor, Diners Club, gradually withered and survives today as a niche brand owned by Citicorp. A similar fate awaited the other major early entrant. Conrad Hilton started Carte Blanche the same year American Express entered. It was soon derided as Carte Rouge, which is why granddaughter Paris is just a hotel heiress.

Avoiding the fate of the failed payment cards requires carefully studying the way a successful catalyst creates value. The Tu-Ba Café in Osaka, Japan, is a new kind of club for singles to find dates. It also provides a very clear example of catalytic reactions at work. Inside the club, men and women sit on opposite sides of a glass divide. If a man sees a woman he likes, he can ask a waiter to carry a "love note" to her. If she's interested, they can get together at the club or go somewhere else for a date. This love club—it is decidedly G-rated—provides value in three ways that are common across catalysts. First, it helps two distinct kinds of customers to find each other. It is a matchmaker. Second, it provides each customer with a number of other customers who may be interested in them. It is an audience builder. Third, it lets customers share a facility for getting together. It is a cost minimizer.

Matchmaking, building audiences, and minimizing the cost of running a community are the core functions of catalysts. Table 1-1 offers a short list of catalyst businesses that perform them in varying proportions to create value for their customers. Let's briefly examine each of these functions.

Matchmakers

Matchmakers aren't just central to the dating and mating business. They are what make much of the economy work.

The Manheim Auto Auction started in its namesake city in Germany in 1945. It now organizes auctions at 124 sites in the United

TABLE 1-1

Types of catalysts

Matchmakers	Audience builders	Cost minimizers
Objective: to facilitate transactions	*Objective: to assemble eyeballs*	*Objective: to increase efficiency*
eBay	*Paris Match*	Palm OS
Yahoo! Personals	Google	Windows
Marché Bastille	Condé Nast Publications	Symbian, Ltd.
MySpace.com	TiVo	Sony PlayStation
Manheim Auto Auction	Reed Elsevier	Xbox
Odaiba	*Wall Street Journal*	SAP enterprise software
NASDAQ	BBC	Linux

States, Europe, and Asia/Pacific as well as on the Internet. Fleet owners, such as automobile rental companies, come to sell their cars to wholesale car dealers at these auctions. Cars come down a conveyor belt. About every forty-five seconds, the hammer falls, ending the bidding process on each car. Manheim doesn't just help buyers and sellers find each other. It also works at keeping everyone honest and brokering any disputes.

Ever since the village market, institutions—and businesses—have helped facilitate transactions between buyers and sellers. Some provide a meeting place where buyers and sellers come and trade with each other. If you live in Paris, you can go to the Marché Bastille on Thursday and Sunday mornings to buy most anything you could want to eat from the many farmer-sellers who have stalls there. If you want to buy or sell stock options, the International Securities Exchange provides a virtual meeting place where trade can occur on line.

Exchange is recognized as the major engine of economic progress throughout human history. It is also one of the oldest forms of human interaction. Unlike love, it involves simple math. Person A would pay $17,000 for a 1988 Porsche 911 coupe. Person B has one that they'd be willing to sell for $14,000. Suppose it costs $1,000 for A and B to find each other and do a deal. Then they have $2,000 of value to split, as shown in figure 1-1.

Exchange between countries, people, and businesses generates these additional values constantly.

FIGURE 1-1

How catalysts create value

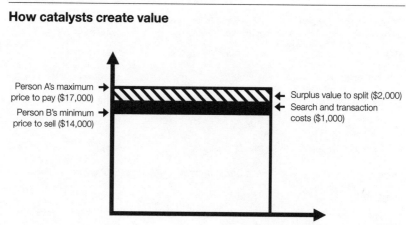

Person A's maximum price to pay ($17,000)
Person B's minimum price to sell ($14,000)

Surplus value to split ($2,000)
Search and transaction costs ($1,000)

Audience Builders

Painted Dreams was the first soap opera. Every weekday an Irish American widow, Mother Moynihan, her daughter, and their young female boarder had a fifteen-minute conversation before the girls went off to their jobs at a hotel. Chicago radio station WGN first aired *Painted Dreams* in 1930. The program was one of many efforts by radio stations in the late 1920s and early 1930s to build an audience of women between the ages of eighteen and forty-nine. Radio stations thought that if they could build such an audience, their program would be attractive to the makers of household cleaners, toiletries, and packaged food that might be good advertising prospects. WGN first approached a detergent manufacturer, then a margarine maker to sponsor the show and ended up with Montgomery Ward & Company, which at the time was the country's largest retailer. *Painted Dreams* was a big hit. And the soap opera became one of the main ways that radio and then television attracted the demographic group sought by Procter & Gamble, General Foods, and other manufacturers of home products.

Advertisers want to buy the attention of consumers who are likely to be interested in their products. They can't do that easily on their own. Media companies buy audiences by providing people with content—a magazine article, the sports section of the daily paper, an Internet search, or a television show, to take a few prominent examples. They also try to aggregate audiences that advertisers particularly want—Gen Yers, suburban moms, or fly fishermen.

Many catalysts build audiences. For advertising-supported media, assembling eyeballs is the main thing they do. But building audiences is a core competency for many others. A woman who goes to the Tu-Ba Café wants a lot of attractive men to be there also. A car wholesaler that goes to Manheim might want to rub elbows with many Fiat sellers to fill out his inventory.

Cost Minimizers

You've just bought *Fight Night Round*, developed by Electronic Arts, for your Xbox. When you insert the DVD into your console, the system will automatically update the machine's operating system. Microsoft has given Electronic Arts the code to do this. That operating system update probably enables your machine to play more complex games. Xbox is constantly adding new features to the code so that you and the games you play can do more.

Having the game developer include this code on the DVD provides Xbox with an efficient means of distributing these updates to users. You benefit because you can play more sophisticated games. Electronic Arts gains because *Fight Night Round* can then rely on the updated code.

Like many catalysts, Xbox is helping its community by building facilities that its members can share. This avoids duplication, lowers costs, and facilitates transactions. Xbox has a block of code, for example, that enables network communication between gamers. Every game manufacturer that wants to allow gamers to interact can use that feature and thereby avoid the cost of writing the code itself. Users get that block of code on their machines, and that feature is then available for every game they want to play. Xbox is based on a software platform. Sharing facilities is one of the key functions performed by companies that make software platforms.

Eliminating duplication and thereby minimizing cost isn't something that only software catalysts do to create value. Diners Club did this with its centralized network for processing transactions among gourmands and restaurants in Manhattan in 1950. The merchant avoided the cost of having its own charge system, while the cardholder avoided having to carry around a card for every eatery. The Manheim Auto Auction is a cost reducer too. Buyers and sellers get to share its facilities and avoid the costs of looking for sellers and buyers spread out around the world. At Mall of America, merchants benefit from plumbing, wiring, and other shared parts of the mall building as well as the free parking that all their customers share. Shoppers benefit from having many merchants close together.

When Two Is Better Than One

To crack the catalyst code, you need to begin by understanding the profound difference between the single-sided businesses that dominate economics and business courses and the multisided ones you will learn more about in this book.

Single-sided businesses cater to just one basic type of customer for each product they sell. Renault makes vehicles for drivers. Deloitte & Touche sells auditing services to public companies. Restaurants provide meals for diners. The pin factory described in Adam Smith's *The Wealth of Nations* was ultimately focused on the customers who needed pins. Of course, there are differences among the customers of these businesses, and many single-sided businesses sell multiple products. Some people want trucks instead of cars and tax services instead of auditing. Even though it may be useful to think of Renault's car and truck customers as two distinct groups, Renault is still single sided because its core business has nothing to do with facilitating interaction between these groups. If it leaves the car business, its truck customers won't automatically vanish, while if the Tu-Ba Café stops trying to attract men, it will not attract women and will go out of business.

One-sided businesses live in a linear world that is well described by the familiar supply chain, shown in figure 1-2. A manufacturer buys parts from various suppliers that in turn have bought parts and raw materials from other suppliers further up the line. It fashions these parts into a finished product. It then often sells this product to wholesale distributors, which in turn supply it to retail stores, which in turn sell it to consumers. Each of these suppliers and distributors charges a price for its services that covers its costs and provides a profit. If the manufacturer can make this chain

FIGURE 1-2

The traditional one-sided business

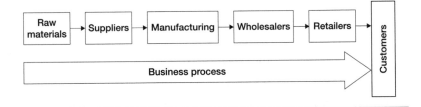

work more efficiently, it can lower its costs, reduce its prices, secure greater sales, and earn higher profits. Dell is just one of the younger firms that have implemented this recipe for success.

The businesses that are the links of the supply chain are basically interchangeable. It doesn't matter to Stop & Shop, an American supermarket chain, who the oat growers are or how many growers there are. It just wants to sell Quaker Oats. Consumers don't care from which or from how many suppliers Renault gets its steel. Nor do car buyers or oatmeal buyers care about each other—so long as there are enough of them to ensure that they get the product at all and that the manufacturers can secure enough scale economies to give them a good price. The manufacturer that stands in the middle of this supply chain has only one side facing customers—the people or businesses to which they provide goods and services.

Catalysts are *multisided*. They cater to two or more basic types of customers who do need each other and who depend on the catalyst to bring them together (see the box "The New Economics of Two-Sided Businesses").

The catalyst and its customer groups form a dynamic system and live in a nonlinear world, as shown in figure 1-3. Changes in

The New Economics of Two-Sided Businesses

William Baxter had the first known academic insight into catalysts.

He was a law professor at Stanford who was known for applying economics to legal problems, particularly in the antitrust arena. He was working on an antitrust case that involved the *interchange fee*—the per-transaction fee paid to banks that issue cards by banks that service merchants that accept cards. He realized that there was no product of value unless the merchant and the cardholder got together and transacted with each other; the interchange fee was used to balance the demand of these two groups. He wrote an article that was published in the *Journal of Law and Economics* in 1983. Baxter went on to become the country's antitrust chief and is most famous for devising the basic

FIGURE 1-3

The catalyst business

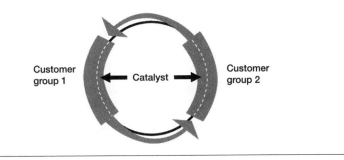

customers of one type affect customers of the other type. The catalyst creates value through a controlled but often powerful reaction among members of the groups in its community. Catalysts all have more than one side facing their customers.

Consider a newspaper. Like a one-sided business, it has a supply chain. It has to buy paper, for example, and it must have distributors. But unlike a linear business, it faces two sets of customers who

legal and economic guidelines the government still uses to evaluate whether mergers are anticompetitive or not.

Almost twenty years later, two world-famous economists based in Toulouse, France—Jean-Charles Rochet and Jean Tirole—were working on a mathematical analysis of interchange fees and extending Baxter's work. They had the deep insight that their models were relevant to many other businesses, such as dating clubs, shopping malls, and video games. They coined the term *two-sided markets* to refer to these industries. Their seminal article on this subject was published in the *Journal of the European Economic Association* in 2003. Since then, the area of two-sided markets has become one of the hottest in economics and is the subject of numerous scholarly papers and conferences. The two-sided markets idea is all about catalysts.

are quite different from each other. On the one side, it faces advertisers, which care about the number and type of readers who view their ads. On the other side, it faces readers, who mainly care about articles about news, sports, arts, and other features. The newspaper provides services to both of these customers and charges them for it.

The newspaper's success depends less on wringing the last penny out of its supply chain and more on nurturing the community of advertisers and readers. It must consider the interdependence of these two groups of customers at every turn. Perhaps it could increase its advertising revenue by lowering its rates and increasing its ads. Increasing the amount of ads relative to other content, however, might turn off readers. Likewise, perhaps it could increase its revenue from readers by raising its subscription and newsstand prices. That would reduce readership and make the paper less attractive to advertisers. This *two-sided* business lies in the middle of swirling forces that connect its two distinct groups of customers. Moreover, some catalysts have more than two sides to consider.

PalmSource, Inc. makes the Palm OS operating system for mobile phones, personal digital assistants, and other handheld computing devices. This operating system provides services to developers that write applications for it, hardware makers that use it to power their handheld devices, and users who buy Palm OS–powered devices. Customers who buy a Palm OS device care about applications such as calendars, digital alarm clocks, or electronic games. Developers care about how many customers have these devices or can get them through device makers. And device makers care about the availability of applications because more applications mean that Palm OS–powered devices will be more desirable to users.

Whenever a business has more than one customer side, the rules of the game change. The business must account for the forces of mutual attraction among these customer sides, and it has to figure out how to start and control the catalytic reaction among them. That leads to an important lesson for wannabe catalysts: you should start the development of your business by carefully identifying the customer groups that value each other and understanding why.

It is often said that to a man with a hammer, the world looks like a nail. Similarly, once some people understand what a catalyst does, all businesses look like catalysts to them. For instance, we sometimes hear that supermarkets are catalysts because they help bring consumers and producers together and profit from doing so. The problem with this view is that producers mainly care about selling merchandise to the supermarket. So long as Stop & Shop pays Procter & Gamble for the Tide laundry detergent it sells, Procter & Gamble does not care about how the grocery store markets itself to customers. For its part, Stop & Shop focuses its energies on getting shoppers into its stores and goes to suppliers to get whatever it needs to sell. The company doesn't have to worry much about *attracting* suppliers.

Contrast supermarkets with high-end art galleries. When someone walks in and buys a painting, the gallery splits the proceeds with the artist. And if the painting doesn't sell, it goes back to the artist. To attract well-heeled art lovers into its showrooms, the gallery has to have art that will appeal to their taste and their pocketbooks. And to offer their paintings, the best artists must believe that the gallery has a good chance of attracting buyers. Galleries are catalysts. They work hard to attract both sides to their platforms.

In many situations, the line between single-sided and multisided businesses isn't always sharp. Single-sided businesses sometimes find success in turning themselves at least partly into catalysts. Wal-Mart started like a traditional retailer. It bought merchandise from suppliers and resold it to its customers. Over the years, though, Wal-Mart has used the massive shelf space it has available in its stores and its efficient sales and distribution system to attract suppliers that want access to Wal-Mart's millions of customers and to induce them to offer unique products that can help entice consumers. Much of the risk for moving merchandise falls back on the manufacturer. Manufacturers whose products don't fly off the shelves fast enough lose access to the Wal-Mart platform. So Wal-Mart has moved some of the way from a one-sided retail distributor model to a two-sided mall model. Many sophisticated supermarkets have moved in the same direction. Table 1-2 provides some detailed examples of one-sided and two-sided businesses as well as some in between.

In many business situations, it is important to choose carefully between a single-sided and a multisided strategy. Some businesses don't have any choice, of course. If you want to be in the heterosexual

TABLE 1-2

Single-sided versus two-sided business

One-sided	Two-sided	One going on two
Kentucky Fried Chicken restaurants buy supplies and make meals for people who come in. Customers don't know or care where the chicken came from, and the poultry farms don't care who eats the chickens.	Edward Lloyd's Coffeehouse in seventeeth-century London brought together businessmen engaging in shipping and underwriters interested in insuring their ventures.	Silicon Valley coffee shops are famous meeting places for entrepreneurs and venture capitalists.
Apple's iPod/iTunes media platform resells music from major publishers to consumers who want to play it on their iPods.	Microsoft's digital media software platform relies on hardware makers to produce digital music players and on content providers to make music available.	Google Video sells digital videos to consumers. It also provides an online exchange where people can post videos and meet buyers who might be interested in those videos.
William H. Smith is an airport bookseller that buys books and magazines from publishers and sells these to consumers who come to its stores.	*Vogue* attracts fashion-conscious readers through its articles and advertising and attracts fashion advertisers that want to reach these readers.	Amazon.com started by selling books to consumers online. About one-third of its revenue now comes from operating an online shopping mall where sellers can transact with buyers.
The Sears card enables shoppers to buy and pay for goods at Sears and other stores affiliated with Sears. Sears signs up cardholders and earns profit by lending them money.	MasterCard operates a global payment card system in which millions of cardholders can transact with millions of merchants.	Wal-Mart issues cards to its customers that can be used at other merchants that belong to the Discover Network.
DIRECTV buys television shows and makes these available to subscribers of its satellite service.	Fox TV buys and develops content that attracts viewers who then attract advertisers.	TiVo offers a service based on a digital video recorder that downloads television shows and allows users to skip over commercials. It is making its subscriber base available to advertisers for inserting long-form advertisements that consumers can play optionally.

dating business, you'd better serve both men and women, and thus you must be a catalyst. But other businesses can choose whether they want to pursue a two-sided strategy. Pay-TV and satellite radio, for example, demonstrated that they could start media companies without relying on advertisers. They recognized and pursued a single-sided strategy. Similarly, the original Palm Pilot relied on a business model that was consciously one sided. Palm made everything from the hardware device, to the applications, to the operating system, and it focused only on selling to end users. It had no relationship with third-party developers and didn't make an effort to cultivate that relationship before it launched its product. But as the Pilot became more popular and the Palm operating system matured, Palm began to court independent software vendors and became a catalyst, bringing users and software developers together.

When firms should be multisided, which customer groups they should serve, when they should outsource, and when they should self-supply are among the critical topics we address in what follows.

Profit Patterns

Sony sold 16.2 million of its PlayStation 2 video game consoles worldwide in 2005.[8] Its game division earned $570 million of profits in 2004.[9] Figuring out where these come from is a more complicated issue for Sony and other catalysts than it is for many businesses. People paid Sony anywhere between $150 and $250 for PlayStation game consoles that year, depending when they bought and what retailer they bought from. Sony didn't make much from consoles directly, since it sells them at close to manufacturing cost. But people bought games for those consoles, and Sony got about $8 per game from the publishers. The hit game *Grand Theft Auto: San Andreas*, by Rockstar Games, alone sold more than 9 million copies.

Given these facts, you might be tempted to conclude that Sony made its profit from games, not consoles. That's right in one sense: if you compare revenue with direct operating costs, the game developers are producing virtually all the profits. But it is wrong in another, more fundamental sense. Those game developers wouldn't have made the investments—and paid the royalties—that generated this much revenue if Sony hadn't persuaded millions of people to buy the consoles. If Sony hadn't made good consoles so inexpensive—if it had tried to make more profits from console sales—it would have killed the goose that laid the golden egg of game royalties.

This way of thinking about the source of profits leads to an important lesson for designing catalyst organizations. At bonus time, which Sony employee should get the fatter check? The woman who is in charge of doing licensing deals with the game developers and who raked in most of the company's profits that year? Or the man who is in charge of the console manufacturing division and who beat the company's goals for selling consoles but still had a small operating loss? Both are important to the success of the business. And the manufacturing head might have contributed more even though his division showed a loss, and he might have made the job of the licensing head quite easy.

Looking across many catalysts reveals clear patterns in how they earn profits. They get revenue by charging customers for coming to the catalytic reaction. Magazines charge subscription fees. Many credit cards charge holders an annual fee. Exchanges often charge traders membership fee, and singles clubs charge an entrance fee. Game console makers charge for the console. (Catalysts are not all in it for the profit. See the box "Catalysts as Nonprofits".)

Catalysts also get revenue by charging customers for participation in interactions. Many just charge for successful interactions. Real estate brokers charge sellers a commission when they complete a transaction. Auction houses often charge a commission to both the buyer and the seller of an expensive painting. Merchants pay a fee whenever a cardholder completes a transaction. Web portals usually charge according to the number of people who click through the ad.

An important pattern is that many catalysts charge some groups prices that are lower than the direct cost of supporting those customers. Often there is no charge at all: the catalyst provides an inducement to join the community or interact with other members of the community. PalmSource charges developers little, American Express gives cardholders a very good deal, and Sony doesn't charge console buyers much. These low prices lead indirectly to profits because they help build a community that supports the catalytic reaction.

Catalysts as Nonprofits

Catalysts aren't always operated by for-profit businesses.

Governments operated some of the oldest catalysts, such as the Roman Forum. Cities and towns still operate markets in part to raise revenues. The ground levels of two major parking garages in Toulouse—at Place des Carmes and Place Victor Hugo—are bustling from the early morning to the early afternoon seven days a week with fishmongers, vegetable sellers, butchers, and others. Governments still produce cash and often have their fingers in checks—two of the leading monetary catalysts.

Associations of businesses sometimes try to develop a pleasant area for merchants and shoppers to come together. The Fifth Avenue Association, established in 1907 in New York City, has made it its mission to maintain the cachet associated with the Fifth Avenue shopping experience. Its antipeddler initiatives and private security and trash collection programs are aimed at attracting and maintaining this area's upscale merchants and shoppers.

Cracking the Catalyst Code

Entrepreneurs that discover opportunities to establish powerful catalytic reactions and exploit those opportunities in creative and disciplined ways can provide tremendous benefits for the agents they bring together and make considerable profits for themselves. But as we have already suggested in this chapter, catalysts follow their own unique patterns of organization and behavior. Like economists who first recognized catalysts for what they are, you will be stymied if you try to analyze or explain catalyst strategies using the conventional tools of strategic analysis. Some of the necessary concepts, such as network effects, have been around for a while.[10] But it has taken significant recent advances, and unlearning old ways of thinking, to figure out what really makes catalysts tick and thrive.

This book will show you how to crack the catalyst code. It will help you identify a community of agents from which it is possible to generate catalytic power. It will describe *two-sided business strategies* that have proved successful in establishing and sustaining profitable catalytic reactions. It will also teach you the revolutionary business principles that will help you implement in new contexts the sophisticated pricing, design, and organizational techniques that some of the greatest catalysts have used to transform markets, provide value for their communities, and make fortunes for themselves.

This book isn't just for entrepreneurs looking to get into new businesses or evolve their current ones. It is also for the many businesses that work with catalysts as part of their communities. Video game makers such as Electronic Arts, for example, have to work with catalysts such as Sony PlayStation. Moreover, if you invest in, report on, work for, or represent an industry that is—or might be— shaped by economic catalysts, this book will reveal the forces that hold catalysts together and sometimes, as with the "dead mall" that no one visits anymore, make their catalytic reactions fade away.

In the course of this explanation, readers who aspire to understand their catalyst partners better or who interact with catalysts in other parts of their lives will learn how these remarkable businesses both create value for society and produce the occasional billionaire. To help readers understand this process, we will begin in the next chapter by examining how catalysts perform their core functions and describing the *catalyst framework,* which lays out the tasks necessary to build a successful catalyst.

2

Build a Catalyst Strategy

Rule No. 1: Never lose money.

Rule No. 2: Never forget rule No. 1.

— WARREN BUFFET

8MINUTEDATING IS THE LEADING PROVIDER OF SPEED dating in the United States. Singles gather at a popular restaurant. They then have eight one-on-one conversations with randomly selected members of the opposite sex. The chats last eight minutes each. After the eighth conversation, the singles can mingle and meet other people. At the end of this session, they can go on a Web site and identify the people they would like to see again. Whenever two people name each other, 8minute Dating puts them into contact so they can arrange a second date on their own. Each speed dater pays roughly $35 for the service, which includes registration, food, and sometimes surprises. As of late 2006, this service operated in more than eighty cities and had completed more than five thousand speed-dating events involving more than two hundred fifteen thousand men and women during its first six years of operation.[1]

Tom Jaffee, who started 8minuteDating in Boston in 2001, has performed three activities to start and sustain his catalytic reaction. He and his partners *build* the catalyst community by getting men and women to come to their events. They don't have a service to offer unless they can get enough men and women to come to the speed-dating event. They *stimulate* interactions between men and women who come to the event through the synchronized dates and then through connecting partners who like each other afterward. They also *govern* the community of men and women through a variety of practices. Couples aren't supposed to seek contact information from prospective partners during the event, for instance, to "keep the conversations comfortable and safe."[2]

These three activities—building, stimulating, and governing—create and sustain most successful catalytic reactions. Google, for example, has gotten advertisers and information seekers to use its technology. It has developed sophisticated methods for increasing the number of people who see an advertisement they care about. It also helps ensure that information seekers get the most relevant information in part by punishing purveyors of information and advertisers that try to game its complex algorithms. Google gave BMW the boot in early 2006 for allegedly trying to manipulate the search results. Likewise, American Express gets merchants and cardholders to use a common device—a plastic card—for making and taking payments. It provides merchants with help on transaction technology and gives cardholders rewards for using their cards to stimulate transactions. And it has rules that protect merchants from the fraudulent use of cards and that give cardholders recourse if the merchant doesn't deliver the goods.

To build communities, catalysts *create a value proposition* through persuasion, pricing, and product design. To stimulate interactions, they *provide information and search methods* that help customers connect with each other effectively. And to govern the community, they *devise rules and standards* that help customers know what is expected of them and limit "bad interactions." Figure 2-1 highlights these catalyst activities. Examining how catalysts have successfully—and unsuccessfully—performed these activities and the

FIGURE 2-1

Catalyst activities

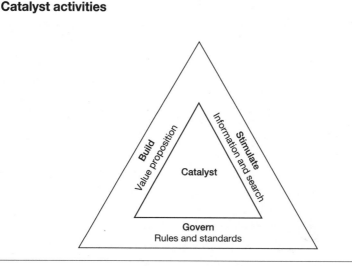

tactics they have used to do so provides fundamental lessons for how to build, stimulate, and govern a profitable catalytic reaction.

Activity 1: Create a Value Proposition

"Man is by nature a social animal," as Aristotle observed in 382 BC.[3] Economic and social transactions bind us together. People, and the businesses they form, are constantly exchanging goods and services and moving them from lower-valued uses to higher-valued ones. No less important, people continually exchange value with each other through love and friendship. Catalysts facilitate these transactions. That is their source of value, their role in the economy, and the fountain from which their profits spring.

Creating Value for Money or Love

Starting at four in the morning, six days a week, more than sixty thousand people come to buy and sell seafood at the Tsukiji Central Wholesale Market in Tokyo. More than 600 billion yen's (about

$5.5 billion) worth of seafood, weighing about one million tons, changes hands at the Tsukiji every year.[4]

Most of the fish consumed by the 8.1 million people who live in the Tokyo metropolitan area passes its way through the Tsukiji—the world's largest fish market. After buyers have had a chance to inspect the fish, bells go off at 6 a.m., and the auctions begin. Buyers and sellers go to designated pits for each variety of fish. A licensed auctioneer, called a *serinin*, conducts a round of bidding every fifteen minutes or so in the pit. Each serinin works for an auction house that has taken fish on consignment to sell.

Much of the fish is sold to traders who resell the fish they purchased at auctions in their own stalls. By going to the auction, they can offer a selection of fish to sushi chefs and others whose needs are too small to buy in bulk at the auctions.[5]

Great value is created by this trading platform. With serinin and auction pits at its heart, the Tsukiji solves an immense coordination and matching problem in a couple of hours. Fish is moved efficiently from those who catch it to those who want to eat it. And this process places each piece of fish in the hands of those who are willing to pay the most for it.

Adam Smith coined the term *the invisible hand* in his 1776 *Wealth of Nations* to describe how "the market" creates value. Ever since, markets have seemed almost metaphysical. In much economic and business writing, the market is seen as an abstraction. The Tsukiji brings home the fact that markets are real. It reeks with the odors of fish and sweat and heavy machinery. Many market institutions, like the Tokyo fish market, are woven into the fabric of the economy.

The Smithian hand isn't that hard to see: you just need to look for the catalysts that make it work. Catalysts have formed over human history to facilitate exchange. Today, they include auction houses like Sotheby's, financial exchanges such as Deutsche Börse, commodities exchanges like the Chicago Board of Trade, online marketplaces like China's Alibaba, and all those shopping malls just off the New Jersey Turnpike. These institutions make markets work.

Exchange achieves what the medieval alchemists couldn't: it creates something from nothing; it serves the proverbial free lunch.[6] Swapping goods among people creates value.

So, too, does finding love. Helping men and women find marriage partners is one of the oldest businesses. In ancient China, the *mei-ren* was like today's investment banker. The family of the prospective groom often retained a matchmaker to find a suitable bride for their son. When the mei-ren found a mutually agreeable match, she negotiated the "deal" between the two families. The matchmaker-cum-negotiator began with an engagement letter and a betrothal gift. Later she worked out the "brideprice" that the groom's family agreed to pay the bride's family. Acceptance of the brideprice, accompanied with a gift document, sealed the deal. The mei-ren then sought agreement on an auspicious marriage date and completed her job by welcoming the bride for the final ceremony.

The Chinese matchmaking system just seems like another form of exchange. But that misses the point that the value of marriage, friendship, and collegiality results from the mutual attraction that humans have for each other and the value they obtain from being with each other. In accepting the match and negotiating the "term sheet" for a marriage transaction, Chinese families considered the benefits of companionship for their child. It wasn't like selling the family ox.

Many societies eventually decided to give boys and girls a greater say in whom they married. Matchmakers started working directly for the partners. Other institutions emerged—from formal balls in nineteenth-century France to singles clubs in 1960s Manhattan. Some consider the turn-of-the-century speed dating the most significant innovation in courtship in many centuries. Others, of course, consider it a sign that Starbucks has raised the caffeine level of a whole generation.

Tactics for Enhancing the Value Proposition

Most catalysts enhance value through three kinds of tactics. These involve developing communities, designing products, and setting prices.

Developing a community. Guy Kawasaki was a great *evangelist* (see the box "The Evolution of 'Evangelist'"). He didn't preach about a higher power or start a church or cure the incurable. This Japanese

American was responsible for creating a modern cult: programmers dedicated to using the Apple Macintosh operating system for developing applications. Today, of course, the Mac has turned into a niche product used by fewer than 4 percent of personal computer users. But better a niche than extinction, the fate of most of Apple's early-1980s rivals. The dedicated followers created by Kawasaki are one reason that Apple survived long enough to create the iPod.

The software evangelist became a staple of the personal computer revolution. Microsoft's evangelists might have been less cool than Apple's but they were more successful at building up a community of developers. Open source evangelists have followed in the Kawasaki tradition of creating an almost cultlike faith in a particular software platform, and that faith is shaking up the computer industry around the world.

THE LESSON

Develop a community as you would develop a congregation. Make customers really feel that they belong to something that is powerful and meaningful for their economic or personal lives.

The Evolution of "Evangelist"

Evangelists can play a critical role in motivating the external "team" in support of the overall success of a catalyst.

The word *evangelist* comes from the Koine Greek word εὐάγγελοσ (*eu-angelos*), meaning "bringer of good news." Its original application was in a religious context, with the "good news" attributed to the preaching and writings of the four Christian Apostles—Matthew, Mark, Luke, and John—and other historical religious figures. The good news was designed to help evangelists build followers and assemble groups of believers who went on to inspire others. It's how many of the world's religions began, and it is why they survive.

In the mid-1980s, Guy Kawasaki coined its use in another, less religious, but perhaps just as powerful, context. This UCLA

Creating communities is one of the major ways catalysts create and capture value. Consider exchanges. When you sell something—be it your house or your collection of Barbie dolls—ultimately you care about getting the best price, net of transactions costs. Despite the fact that hundreds of people may see your home on a multiple listing service or thousands of potential buyers might see your doll collection, an online auction service is only a means to an end. You are only going to transact with one person. But the more interested potential buyers, the better the price you will get on average.

Real estate agents, for example, have joined forces to create multiple listing services that advertise properties to other real estate agents (and the buyers who have contacted them) throughout a geographic area. The U.S. National Association of Real Estate Brokers has developed Realtor.com, which provides a convenient online listing service.

THE LESSON

Give each member of one customer group access to many members of the other customer group. To sustain a catalytic

---

MBA graduate was hired by Apple to persuade software and hardware developers to write for the Macintosh platform. Sounds easy, but consider the challenge at that time: IBM was selling ten PCs to every one of Apple's Macs. But for Guy, it was easy.

As he says, "When I saw what a Macintosh could do, the clouds parted and the angels started singing. For four years I evangelized Macintosh to software and hardware developers and led the charge against world-wide domination by IBM."[7] Just like any evangelist, he believed in his "cause." And just like any evangelist, he got others to believe too. Apple's net sales grew from $983 million in 1983 to $2.661 billion in 1987, almost tripling in four years. In this capacity, Kawasaki was engaged in more than sales promotion or public relations. He was aligning the interests of different groups in the Apple platform community.

reaction, two-sided businesses have to build audiences for each side.

Designing products. Catalysts always provide a physical or virtual place for members of the community to get together. Not surprisingly, the words *club* or *platform* are commonly used to describe many of the businesses that we now understand are catalysts.

Consider some popular meeting places. Almost overnight, My-Space.com became *the* online meeting place for sixteen- to thirty-four-year-olds. The Chicago Board of Trade has twenty-one trading pits, where buyers and sellers exchange various commodities, including corn, soybeans, and wheat. Each pit is roughly 1,100 square feet, although the soybean pit is slightly larger. Mall of America has 2.5 million square feet, where retailers and shoppers get together to transact. Eurofit's Club House in Paris has about 500 square feet, where many singles dance, drink, and mingle.

Some meeting places provide indirect contact between members of the community. Cardholders and merchants "met" in the Diners Club settlement facility in the Empire State Building in Manhattan. Sifting through paper slips, employees paid the stores and billed the shoppers.

With computers and communication, virtual meeting places are increasingly common. The eBay community of buyers and sellers "meet" on a server farm and are connected to this platform mainly through the Internet.

Designing these meeting places well is critical, since evangelizing can only do so much to build a community. Some of the dotcoms had truly memorable advertising, but they failed because even great advertising can't sell a weak value proposition. Apple and Microsoft spend a lot on evangelization, but they spend even more on developing powerful operating systems that are attractive to both end users and application developers. Their evangelists have good products to sell.

THE LESSON

Design your physical or virtual meeting place so it can serve as the core of a value proposition attractive to both groups.

Setting prices. Getting prices right is absolutely critical for catalysts. If you get them wrong, you won't even get your business off the ground. Remember, your prices have to be set at a level that will entice enough customers from each side and in the right proportions to create a value proposition for consumers on both sides. If you don't, neither side will value participating in your catalytic reaction. And unless you get the right prices, you won't generate profit. To understand how to price, you have to leave behind much of what you may have learned about ordinary, single-sided businesses.

There is no set model for catalyst pricing. Many have followed the credit card model of (+/0)—charge one group of customers and let the other group into the "club" for free or at least for less than cost. Shopping malls don't charge customers to get in and may even give them free parking and occasional entertainment. Apple doesn't charge developers for using the extremely valuable code in Mac OS X Tiger. You can google for free.

Pricing discussions in traditional business economics and marketing classes usually focus almost exclusively on single-sided businesses. These firms, textbooks tell us, look for the optimal markup over marginal cost for each product they sell. There is nothing wrong with this analysis, as far as it goes, but it is seriously incomplete for two-sided businesses. Frank McNamara could have gotten people to pay something for the card that was the key to his Diners Club. Fewer people would have joined, of course, but he would have had more profits from cardholders. But he'd have taken a hit from merchants. With fewer cardholders, some merchants wouldn't have gone through the hassle of joining the club and accepting the card. And it gets worse. Diners Club would then have been less attractive to cardholders, with fewer places where they could use their cards. Some would decline the card. And the downward spiral would continue.

Similarly, eBay charges a flat percentage rate to sellers who list items on its auction site, but browsing and shopping are open to anyone with an Internet connection without charge. When eBay raises its seller fees, some merchants howl. Many might decide to stop listing items on eBay, auction them on a rival site, or simply start their own Web site. But in some cases, the price increases are intended to influence seller behavior. According to eBay's CEO, higher selling fees mean fewer lousy products get put up for sale, improving the overall quality of the site for shoppers. This, in turn, benefits high-quality sellers by attracting more buyers.

THE LESSON

Focus on balancing the prices for all sides. Two-sided businesses have to get both sides to the reaction and in the right proportions. They have to keep the two sides in the right balance. To do that, they may have to lower prices to one customer group below incremental cost to get enough volume to attract the other customer group. There's a lot more to pricing, as we'll see in chapter 4.

Activity 2: Facilitate Search and Provide Information

Society wouldn't need catalysts if everyone knew who they should match up with for a profitable exchange or a wonderful relationship and if it were easy to find that match. Perfect information and costless search would lead to nirvana with nary a two-sided business to be found. Catalysts abound because search is hard and information is costly; they assist with the difficult process of search and help provide information to the members of their communities.

Finding the Perfect Match

Google has made search a big business and a hot technology. It has many competitors trying to find better techniques for finding things among the vast amount of digital information on hard drives around the world. But search has been at the heart of catalysts for several millennia.

Village markets often do little more to aid search than grouping the vegetable stands in one area and the fish stalls in another.

Men and women just seek each other out at nightclubs, though by going to a particular club, they may increase their odds of finding the sort of person they want. Similarly, American advertisers and readers find each other in part by choosing among *Cosmopolitan, Outdoor Life,* and thousands of other publications, depending on who they are looking for.

The first recorded auction involved men bidding for marriage partners in Babylon in 500 BC. The most beautiful woman was offered first, then the next, and so on. As the auction continued, some women had to offer a dowry to attract a mate. Ancient Buddhist monks used to raise money by auctioning the possessions of colleagues who had died. As we've seen, everything from fine art to fresh fish is subject to auctions organized by catalysts. EBay has brought auctions to the masses. Many goods are sold on eBay through a second-price auction. Buyers can keep entering higher bids until the auction ends. The product goes to the highest bidder but at a price equal to the second-highest bid.

Modern financial exchanges use different mechanisms. On some exchanges, buyers and sellers submit orders of various kinds electronically, and computers match them with each other. This approach to helping buyers and sellers search for each other works well when transactions are frequent (as for shares of, say, Citicorp stock), while auctions often make sense for infrequent transactions (as for paintings by Rembrandt). On other exchanges, market makers or specialists provide liquidity by continuously posting prices at which they will buy or sell. They profit from the difference between their buying and selling prices—the so-called bid-ask spread.

The dating and mating business uses many search techniques. These range from the "go mingle" approach of modern nightclubs and nineteenth-century balls, to the peripatetic village matchmaker, to computerized matching. Speed dating takes the randomness (not to mention the stress) out of mingling and the time out of searching. People decide whether they like or dislike another person based on a brief encounter. Rather than suffering through a meal with a date you've rejected before the appetizer, with speed dating you can make a decision in a few minutes. Rather than waiting for a call, you can quickly find out whether there is mutual interest shortly after the session.

THE LESSONS

Search has some mathematical features for which catalyst entrepreneurs and their investors should account.

More is good—up to a point. You are more likely to find a good offer or a good mate if you consider more alternatives. Search takes time and money, though. Catalysts need to build a large enough community to make sure that participants have enough choices.

More is bad—after a point. Catalysts with a physical meeting place face two problems in increasing the size of the community. Letting more people in eventually leads to congestion. That makes it harder to search. Expanding the size of the meeting place limits congestion but makes search more time consuming. Catalysts face diminishing returns to size when it comes to search. At some point, the extra value you will get from looking at more possibilities will be outweighed by the extra cost of looking. That's one of the reasons why most of us don't look at all possible houses we could buy, jobs we could get, or partners we could romance.

Sorting helps search. Efficient search requires narrowing down the possibilities to minimize wasted effort. Catalysts need to provide sorting mechanisms to do this. The Tsukiji Central Wholesale Market, the Manheim Auto Auction, and *Cosmopolitan* all help their customers narrow down their choices. The Tsukiji does this by having different fish sold at different stands, *Cosmo* by having content that attracts a certain kind of woman to whom certain advertisers want to sell. Table 2-1 summarizes these principles and their implications.

Providing Information

Pierre Omidyar started an online flea market called Auction-Web in 1995. An early Web page listed Marky Mark underwear, a cast iron hook and ladder truck, and a rose bowl. Buyers and sell-

TABLE 2-1

Catalyst search principles

Insight	Implications
People want choices.	The community has to be large enough to offer participants enough choices.
Search takes time and money.	There are diminishing returns inherent in offering too much choice.
Sorting helps narrow the possibilities.	Catalysts must help customers search efficiently.

ers operated on the honor system since there was no way for this one-man operation to police whether they really were Marky's drawers or whether the high bidder for the rose bowl reneged. Most people behaved well, but some didn't. There was a lack of information about buyers and sellers.

A year later Omidyar created the Feedback Forum. People could praise or complain about their transaction partners. Auction-Web evolved into eBay. After you complete a transaction, you are asked to rate the buyer or seller on the opposite side of the transaction on a five-star scale and provide any comments. The scores for buyers and sellers are accumulated across all their transactions and posted prominently. This provides valuable information about the reliability of prospective transaction partners and serves to police the community.

Other catalysts provide information by directly policing their communities. Rather than charging more, for instance, popular dating venues select people from those in line to ensure quality. The more stringent such controls, the more confidence people can have in the quality of the communities in these clubs.

THE LESSON

Grease your physical or virtual meeting place with reliable information to make it easier for customers to find the best exchanges and companions.

Activity 3: Devise Rules and Standards

Catalysts create communities, and communities need governance lest they devolve into anarchy. While people benefit from each other through exchanges and relationships, they also hurt each other through fraud, theft, or free riding on the efforts of others. Catalysts have to encourage people to help each other and prevent them from harming each other. They enact rules and impose punishments, and they promulgate standards of behavior.

Platform Rules

Just as the market system would collapse if governments didn't enforce contract, property, and other laws, catalytic reactions generally require that participants be able to trust each other.

The most sophisticated rules and regulations may be those employed by organized exchanges. All exchanges have rules against *front-running*, for instance. This practice occurs when a broker with a large purchase order from a customer buys on his own account before executing the customer order, which drives the price up slightly, and then sells on his own account and pockets the resulting profit. Banning this practice directly harms brokers, but it makes buyers more confident that they are getting the best price possible, and thereby enhances the exchange's overall value proposition.

Rules governing exchanges are hardly a modern invention. The *argentarius* organized and regulated the ancient Roman auctions. The tenth-century fairs in Bruges, Champagne, and other northern European cities had strict rules. Someone inspected the goods on offer and condemned the inferior or spoiled. The Tsukiji and Manheim have regulators with similar roles.

MasterCard has rules that govern the appearance of cards issued by members to provide some uniformity for the shared brand, as well as to prevent members from using the brand inappropriately. The system also has rules that address disputed transactions. Acquirers would have an incentive to favor their customers (merchants) in a dispute, while issuers would favor their customers (cardholders). The system's rules attempt to find a balance between these competing interests, to increase the attractiveness of the system as a whole.

THE LESSON

Catalysts must have rules that prevent members of their communities from taking unfair advantage of each other.

Standards of Engagement

Until about the seventh century BC, exchanges between buyers and sellers were generally based on barter—four oxen for a female slave is one transaction described by Homer. More sophisticated traders could exchange precious metals in whatever shapes and sizes they had. Lydia, an ancient state in what is now Turkey, is often given credit for developing coins made of gold and silver in fixed amounts. These gold and silver coins provided a unit of account and an easy method of exchange. By creating a standard, the Lydians facilitated exchange across a region that eventually extended west to Italy and east to Persia.

Money is a catalyst business. The ancient city-states earned profits from it by debasing their currency—reducing the amount of precious metal in their coins over time. Modern governments do this more efficiently by printing money and driving inflation. But money feeds a catalytic reaction only so long as buyers and sellers are willing to use and hold it. The coins of many ancient city-states failed to become standards because their value fell over time as they were debased. The Athenian drachma reigned for four centuries over a good portion of southern Europe and eastern Asia because it developed a reputation for having consistent silver content.

Modern payment networks develop standards through rules, regulations, and branding. Cardholders know they can use their American Express cards at all merchants that post the Amex logo. As part of its contract with merchants, American Express requires that merchants accept all American Express cards. Merchants know that American Express will reimburse them for the charge if they accept an Amex card for payment. Amex also lays out the ground rules for situations in which merchants or cardholders dispute a bill.

Standards are critical strategies for other catalysts. Windows is valuable to developers because they know that more than 90 percent of personal computer users have this operating system installed on their computer or are likely to buy a computer that uses Windows. It is valuable to users because they know that there are many applications that will work with Windows and many developers that are continuing to write new programs for it.

As this example suggests, standards are often about shaping mutually consistent expectations. A developer anticipates having many users if it writes for Windows; a user anticipates many applications if she buys a computer with Windows. A buyer anticipates that many sellers will take his Visa card for payment; a seller anticipates that many buyers will present a Visa card for payment. Shoppers anticipate when they go to an upscale mall that they will find stores like Williams-Sonoma, and merchants that rent space at upscale malls anticipate getting well-heeled customers. Manhattan singles going to the Texas-themed Rodeo Bar expect to meet a different crowd than those going to the fashionable Bungalow 8.

THE LESSON

Standards provide a way of creating a virtual meeting place, shaping expectations, and building a community.

Competition Among Catalysts

Even catalysts that effectively perform the three activities outlined so far cannot avoid a fundamental threat: competition. Most vie for customers with other catalysts or single-sided firms. And just as pioneering catalysts swept away settled industries, so do today's established catalysts face serious threats from the new and the unknown. As they implement their strategies for creating value for their communities and profit for themselves, they must look all around for rivals set on disrupting their plans and taking their customers.

We will examine the nature of competition among catalysts in greater depth in chapter 7. For the moment, however, it is worth highlighting some unique features of competition faced by catalysts as we think about the strategies involved in building a successful one. One is the possibility that customers use two or more competing catalysts at the same time. Economists refer to this as *multihoming*. We see this situation all the time in competition among broadcast networks: advertisers use multiple networks, and consumers watch multiple networks. On the other hand, most computer users *single-home*: they use either a Mac or a Windows PC, not both. The easier it is for customers to multihome, the easier it is for them to switch vendors as catalysts' prices and products change.

A second unique feature is that catalysts may face competition from firms with very different business models. We have already mentioned that advertiser-supported broadcast radio stations have come to face competition from satellite radio providers that have subscription revenues. Similarly, *intersecting catalysts*, which serve different groups with different business models, may find themselves fighting for the business of one of these groups. Local newspapers charge all classified advertisers and sell to readers below cost. Craigslist, in contrast, generally allows consumers to post ads for free and charges only employers. Anyone can browse its online listings for free. When craigslist started stealing classified advertising dollars from city newspapers, some of the papers responded by building their own online ad sites. The nature of the competition a catalyst faces is critical in determining the best way to respond through the value proposition, product design, pricing, and community governance.

Building a Successful Catalyst: A Framework

Entrepreneurs who discover opportunities to establish powerful catalytic reactions and exploit those opportunities in creative and disciplined ways can provide tremendous benefits for the agents they bring together and make considerable profits for themselves. Those who pursue a compelling value proposition, set down clear rules and standards, and offer sophisticated search and information capabilities might well be on their way to a successful catalyst. But not always. AltaVista, one of the earlier online search engines, seemed to be a leader in what was widely recognized as a rapidly growing field. But rather than specializing in what it did best, under Compaq's ownership it tried to turn itself into a Yahoo! clone. It didn't have any advantages that could dislodge market leader Yahoo!, and at the same time its "beefed-up" home page alienated its old users. Without enough value to attract viewers or advertisers, its business floundered, and its technology was sold off. Laggard Google focused on search technology and uncovered the advertising-supported search model that has powered its growth.

To take another example, Chemdex, which was considered one of the most promising B2Bs in the late 1990s, saw profits in establishing an electronic exchange where biotech companies and their suppliers could meet. It had the right prices to attract 24,000 suppliers with 1.7 million products.[8] Unfortunately, it didn't have a good value proposition for the other side of the market. Most biotech companies cared much more about the reliability of their suppliers than the price for many of their products. Getting a critical reagent a couple of days late, or one that was defective, could be very expensive indeed. To deal with this risk, biotech firms liked long-term personal relationships rather than the anonymous click and buy offered by a Web site. Fleetingly valued at $10 billion, Chemdex followed thousands of other misguided but momentarily highly valued enterprises into oblivion in late 2000.

Successful catalysts don't magically take shape. They need a carefully constructed framework that serves as a guide or road map as entrepreneurs build the business. But while all catalysts must deal with more or less the same questions, the answers are extraordinarily diverse. The forces that attract the customer groups, the nature of their demand, technology, and the competitive landscape are just some of the factors that distinguish one catalyst from another.

The common denominator for catalysts is that they facilitate interactions among distinct customer groups that need each other. NASDAQ helps buyers and sellers of stock find each other.[9] The Yahoo! Personals do the same for people looking for dates and mates. *Nikita*, a Japanese magazine for young women, helps advertisers of hip fashions find women who want that style and helps those women learn more about hip products. Mac OS X Tiger provides programming services that help Mac developers and users transact with each other at lower costs.

Each of these catalysts has a dominant function. NASDAQ is mainly a matchmaker just like the Tsukiji Central Wholesale Market and 8minuteDating. *Nikita* mainly builds audiences as do Google and Fox TV. Mac OS X Tiger is focused primarily on providing efficient programming services to developers and users; the same is true for the Palm OS and Symbian, a widely used software platform used on mobile phones. None of these catalysts is a purebred, though. NASDAQ builds audiences and provides a trading platform that minimizes the cost of trading. *Nikita* specializes in a particular match: between a certain kind of young woman and the products she likes to buy. And it makes it cheaper, especially for advertisers, to find those women. The Mac OS builds audiences of Mac users that it makes available to Mac developers and vice versa.

With this complexity in mind, we have created a catalyst framework, shown in figure 2-2, that is flexible enough to accommodate the wide variety that one finds in catalysts while at the same time presenting the six fundamental elements that are essential for a catalyst to succeed. In the chapters that follow, we will probe more deeply into each one of these elements, identifying the main tasks in each that contribute toward building a successful catalyst.

Identify platform communities. Successful catalysts know who needs whom and why. That is, they have deep knowledge of how, where, and when their different customer groups need each other; how these groups interconnect; and how they can most efficiently and effectively employ the two-sided tactics to facilitate those interconnections. Much of the initial success of Diners Club payment cards was due to founder Frank Mc-Namara's intimate knowledge of both sides of the market. Finding out who needs whom and why becomes the critical knowledge to launch a catalyst. Once that platform community is understood, it becomes much easier to evaluate existing or emerging competition and to design a business model that serves all sides of the market.

Establish the pricing structure. Pricing is a critical function to attract and balance the different catalytic agents. Successful

FIGURE 2-2

The catalyst framework

Identify the platform community	Establish a pricing structure	Design the catalyst for success	Focus on profitability	Compete strategically with other catalysts	Experiment and evolve
• Identify distinct groups that need each other	• Set separate prices for access and usage	• Attract multiple customer groups that need each other	• Study industry history	• Understand the dynamics of catalyst competition	• Know when to be first— and when to follow
• Determine why and how much they need each other	• Set prices to balance demand from two sides	• Promote interactions	• Use forecasts to enhance profitability	• Look for competition from different business models	• Control growth
• Evaluate who else is serving the community	• Price to grow slowly— at first	• Minimize transaction costs	• Anticipate competitor actions	• Leverage to attack	• Protect your back
• Compare a multisided business model with a single-sided one	• Pay customers to belong— sometimes	• Design for evolution	• Align interests internally and externally	• Consider cooperation	• Plan for what's next
	• Price for long-term profits				• Look out for the cops
Find out who needs whom— and why	**Shape participation and maximize profits**	**Draw customers and facilitate interactions**	**Visualize path toward long-term profit**	**Challenge existing catalysts and react to new catalyst threats**	**Pursue evolutionary strategy for growth**

catalysts set prices according to who needs whom the most and not the typical cost-plus model, or value-added pricing, or penetration pricing as other marketers do. They can't insist on making profits from every group. They have to get both sides on their platform and get them on in the right proportions. Mall of America could charge people for getting into its vast complex of stores and entertainment. But it found more profits in building up traffic and capturing its share of the value-added through rent charged to merchants. For these reasons, getting the pricing right needs to be an early goal of any catalyst business.

Design the catalyst for success. The decision of customers to participate in a catalyst business will depend in large measure on how well you can attract them and how easy and alluring it is to join. Whether physical or virtual, the place where customers meet must be safe, secure, easy to reach, and easy to navigate. More importantly, successful platforms compel the distinct groups of customers to interact with each other. That's the secret of 8minuteDating, which takes the muss, fuss, and stress out of meeting people. *Vanity Fair* does this in a different way. Its advertisers want people to look at their ads, so the magazine encourages "interaction" by spreading articles across its pages, thereby making readers flip through more of it. Readers benefit, even if they are annoyed, because attracting more advertisers enables *Vanity Fair* to afford to lower its subscription price and/or provide more content that readers like. And the importance of security is one reason why card systems are taking identify theft so seriously. The ultimate goal is to promote the interaction among different groups of people.

Focus on profitability. Every catalyst needs to examine and anticipate how it will generate profits. Setting up a catalytic reaction between two or more sides of a market is a difficult and impressive feat. But it is often not enough to sustain a business. Successful catalysts learn from the history of a business about what has worked—and what hasn't. They have to imagine where profit might come from under different scenarios, depending upon how the business evolves. They have to anticipate moves by competitors and plan how they will respond. And they need to recognize that profit requires constantly making all the parts of the catalyst community—including their own employees—have a strong stake in having the entire business thrive, even if each part of the community is focused on only a narrow part of the catalyst business. If the circulation people at *Vogue* raise prices because their bonuses depend on profits from subscribers, they may make it much harder for the people across the hall to sell the advertising on which the whole venture depends.

Compete strategically with other catalysts. No matter how well a catalyst pursues its strategy, and no matter how innovative that strategy, it will almost always face competition sooner or later. Competition may come from other similar catalysts, from existing businesses that themselves have been threatened by the catalyst, and from new ideas and technology that give rise to single-sided businesses or catalysts that can transform a market or industry. This is no theoretical threat. Many catalyst businesses that were thriving in 1995 had become threatened a decade later. Understanding potential competitors requires examining the special dynamics of catalyst competition that are relevant only in two- and multisided businesses. Microsoft, the world's largest software manufacturer, with a legion of the most sophisticated software developers, found itself threatened by open source software that was developed by hobbyists working online. Because catalysts, in recent years, have been responsible for rapid-fire innovation, entrepreneurs will need to anticipate new threats while wondering how their own catalyst business can evolve to upset someone else's business.

Experiment and evolve. Catalysts should be nimble enough to plan for long-term growth and be ready to adapt to changing environments. They need to recognize when they need to lead—and when being a follower is advantageous. They need to grow deliberately, experimenting and evolving their prices, products, and services. Even once they are established, a smart catalyst knows how to watch for competitive threats and anticipate what is next in the marketplace. Starting from a start-up search engine company, Google has evolved into an industry leader with diverse service offerings. Google initially planned to license its search technology to other Web sites. It wasn't until 2000 that it began charging for text-based ads placed alongside search results. Two years later, Google moved over to pay-per-click advertising—charging advertisers only when a potential customer clicks on an ad. "Paid search" was not Google's innovation, but it was superbly applicable to what was fast becoming the world's leading search engine. It was a model of an evolutionary catalyst.

The following six chapters will each be devoted to one of these elements in the catalyst framework. Our goal is to show how the three fundamental activities outlined in this chapter can be built into a successful strategy. The result, we hope, will be not only a guide to building a successful business but also an analytical framework that can be used to shed light on the strategies driving the most dynamic companies in the world.

3

Identify the Catalyst Community

But what we have to learn is that we

cannot do everything ourselves.

—Vinton Cerf

In 1796, several physicians, struck by the lack of availability of medical care for the poor, established the Boston Dispensary. Benefactors, including Paul Revere and Sam Adams, provided funding for tickets that were distributed to the needy. The recipients could use these tickets for treatment in their homes from doctors who were affiliated with this centralized facility. Doctors then turned these tickets in to the Boston Dispensary to obtain their pay. A $5 donation provided two people with care for a year.

The Boston Dispensary helped put together three groups that needed each other: doctors who couldn't work for free, sick people who couldn't afford treatment, and charitable people who wanted to help out. By reducing and controlling disease, it also made Boston a better place to live.

The Tufts–New England Medical Center descended directly from this early medical catalyst. Located today steps from its historic site, now near Boston's Chinatown, Tufts is one of the world's leading medical facilities and academic health centers. It cares for all classes of people. Though still a nonprofit entity, it is very much a business. Instead of relying on donors to buy tickets, it mainly depends on insurers to pay claims.

Tufts, along with many other hospitals and medical centers, has created a platform for doctors and patients. The result is a catalyst business that successfully brings together different groups with interdependent interests. In fact, most doctors at Tufts aren't employees of the medical center; they have their own practices. The medical center has to convince them that they should use Tufts for surgery and other procedures that they can't perform in their own offices. Tufts gets them on board its platform by providing a facility that is valuable for them and for their patients. It also provides lucrative financial inducements to star doctors who have particular specialties that can help attract patients as well as other doctors. In 2005, Tufts affiliated with the largest group of primary care physicians in New England as a way to provide greater services to its patient community, attract more patients to its facilities, and thus attract other doctors with complementary practices who wanted to serve those patients. Charitable giving remains important for this catalyst but now accounts for only a modest percentage of its budget.

Like many other important innovations, the catalyst community of doctors, patients, and donors is obvious in hindsight. This chapter aims to provide some foresight. We will see how successful catalysts, such as Tufts Medical Center, pursue the most fundamental element in the catalyst framework: identifying platform communities (see figure 3-1).

To do this, catalyst builders have to map a possible community of groups that need each other and determine whether it is possible to create value for members of all the groups.

This element invariably begins with an intellectual exercise. Aspiring catalysts must start with some insight about how people or businesses could obtain greater value by getting together in some way. This process begins by identifying a problem whose solution will

FIGURE 3-1

The catalyst framework: identify the platform community

Identify the platform community	Establish a pricing structure	Design the catalyst for success	Focus on profitability	Compete strategically with other catalysts	Experiment and evolve
• Identify distinct groups that need each other	• Set separate prices for access and usage	• Attract multiple customer groups that need each other	• Study industry history	• Understand the dynamics of catalyst competition	• Know when to be first— and when to follow
• Determine why and how much they need each other	• Set prices to balance demand from two sides	• Promote interactions	• Use forecasts to enhance profitability	• Look for competition from different business models	• Control growth
• Evaluate who else is serving the community	• Price to grow slowly— at first	• Minimize transaction costs	• Anticipate competitor actions	• Leverage to attack	• Protect your back
• Compare a multisided business model with a single-sided one	• Pay customers to belong— sometimes	• Design for evolution	• Align interests internally and externally	• Consider cooperation	• Plan for what's next
	• Price for long-term profits				• Look out for the cops
Find out who needs whom— and why	**Shape participation and maximize profits**	**Draw customers and facilitate interactions**	**Visualize path toward long-term profit**	**Challenge existing catalysts and react to new catalyst threats**	**Pursue evolutionary strategy for growth**

make people or businesses better off. The Boston physicians began by identifying a crisis that needed to be resolved: the lack of medical care for the poor in Boston. They developed the Boston Dispensary to solve that problem. The various groups that ultimately relied on the dispensary—doctors, patients, and charitable citizens—all existed long before it was established. But the creation of this special catalyst community required the initial recognition that there was no natural way for them to come together—or at least that a much better way would be valuable. The key, therefore, to identifying a catalyst community is to understand why a catalyst is needed in the first place.

Once that problem is recognized, entrepreneurs interested in unleashing and profiting from a catalytic reaction should pursue four tasks to establish a viable community. These four tasks constitute the core of this first element of the framework:

1. Identify distinct groups that need each other.

2. Determine why and how much they need each other.

3. Evaluate who else is serving the community.

4. Make sure that a multisided business model is better than a single-sided one.

Task 1: Identify Distinct Groups That Need Each Other

Anyone considering creating a catalyst needs to embark on an exploratory expedition to determine the boundaries of the possible community. It is best to sweep wide across the landscape and then narrow the quest before staking out a specific claim. The search must focus on groups that have some attraction for each other.

The attraction doesn't have to be mutual. Boston physicians weren't generally concerned about caring for the poor, but the benefactors were. The dispensary developed the ticket program to bring the three groups together. Similarly, most consumers aren't much attracted to advertisers. The media bribe people with content to deliver them to advertisers.

Often, though, the attraction is reciprocal. That is obvious for the buyers and sellers assembled by exchanges, such as the Tsukiji, Tokyo's fish market, and for the people looking for love or companionship brought together by matchmakers like 8minuteDating, which we described in the last chapter. It is a bit less evident for the customers assembled by businesses that we don't ordinarily think of as exchanges or matchmakers. Shoppers and stores are drawn to each other at shopping malls. For software platforms, application developers and users are attracted to one another.

It is worth looking in several directions to determine who may need each other so much that it may make economic sense to start a catalyst.

Matchmakers and Exchanges

This exploration is straightforward for simple exchanges and matchmakers. They look for communities of buyers and sellers, or seekers of companions, to bring together. Historically, many of these basic catalysts have built small communities of people and businesses that might be attracted to each other. The village matchmaker could scour for mates only so far from her base. From society balls, to church socials, to nightclubs, smaller venues seem to work better in this business.

Simple exchanges and matchmakers often specialize by searching for communities that aren't being served by other catalysts. An art gallery might concentrate, for example, on modern sculptures on consignment. DoveBid, Inc., the industrial auction site, focuses on auctioning the assets of bankrupt companies, including most famously the five-foot steel *E* that once graced the entrance to Enron's Houston headquarters. The Core Club, opened in Manhattan in 2005, is a platform for bringing together wealthy and influential people. It charged one hundred founding members $100,000 each to join. Another two hundred "movers and shakers"—drawn from the arts, business, and politics—paid $55,000 for the chance to rub elbows with others whom they hope are at least as wealthy and influential as they.[1]

For well-developed catalyst industries like exchanges and matchmaking, there is a simple lesson for identifying a community:

THE LESSON

Look for groups that other catalysts haven't put together and groups that could get together more easily at a specialized (real or virtual) meeting place.

The Internet has made it possible to develop larger communities of people. It provides a virtual meeting place that can handle almost limitless crowds. And related technologies make it easier to search for matches among very large groups of people. YouTube, for example, enables people to upload, view, and share video clips through its Web site. In July 2006, the company, started by three early employees of PayPal, announced that 100 million clips are viewed each day on its site and 65,000 new videos are uploaded each day. Most of the connections between people with videos and those who want to watch them would never have been made without the emergence of a platform such as this Web site—the tenth most popular on the Web as of September 2006.[2] (Google bought YouTube for $1.65 billion in late 2006.)

Part of the power of the Internet is in helping catalysts identify many small groups of individuals who want to get together. If you love playing three-dimensional chess, you can set up a group on MySpace.com to attract adversaries, and MySpace.com can help advertisers find people who play 3-D chess (see the box "Meet Me at MySpace"). And for those who collect antique credit cards, it is

Meet Me at MySpace

Once upon a time, and not all that long ago, meeting new people was something that was done face-to-face. For those of us who were born before 1966, that is still pretty much the way it is done. Enter the MySpace Generation, those 54 million young people between the ages of sixteen and twenty-nine, who, in addition to shaping fashion, technology, and retail trends, are redefining the way social networking is done, replacing face-to-face networking with interactions in cyberspace.[3]

MySpace.com is not the only online social networking site but is perhaps the most famous one. Established by Tom Anderson and Chris DeWolfe in 2003, MySpace.com was originally designed as a place for musicians to post their music and where fans could chat about it. In the first year, Anderson, himself a musician, managed to convince his Hollywood network to join his online community. As of August 2006, some 100 million MySpace.com members worldwide—as diverse as film and music celebrities, wannabe rock stars, aspiring actors, and average teens—log on every day to connect with their friends, post comments, share stories, and meet new people.[4] MySpacers say that they check their bulletin boards as often as they check their e-mail accounts.

hard to beat eBay for finding sellers. The dot-com matchmakers provide a way for many disparate groups to find each other.

Exchanges have sought scale economies that permit reaching larger communities centuries before the Internet. In 1698, the London Stock Exchange (LSE) began in Jonathan's Coffeehouse in Change Alley. In 2005, more than fifteen thousand stocks and bonds were traded on this exchange, and there were 89 million transactions that year.[5] Although the exchange has moved into larger quarters over its three-century history, it has achieved this scale mainly by developing a community of interrelated businesses. These include investors, brokers and dealers, market makers, and

Interaction among members is facilitated in a number of ways. Members can post a list of their "heroes" and request comments; there are sections that allow members to list where they work and went to school; and there are bulletin boards where friends can post comments about their friends—and their friends' friends.

According to comScore Media Metrix, as of mid 2006, MySpace.com ranked second in the entire U.S. Internet in terms of total page views.[6] And in September 2006 it accounted for 15.4 percent of all advertisements viewed online, a feat all the more impressive since MySpace.com forbids pop-up ads and spyware, which would monitor what members watch.[7] Andersen seeks to make advertising so subtle that its members don't distinguish it from content.

In July 2005, Rupert Murdoch's News Corporation bought MySpace.com for $580 million. His plan is to expand this popular meeting place internationally and to turn it into a full-blown portal, offering free video downloads, a branded instant messenger client, and even voice capabilities. For now, what revenue it has is generated by its advertisers. Obviously, the potential for attracting even more advertisers and more advertising revenue seems significant. The challenge for MySpace.com now is to balance the interests of both of its sides—members and advertisers—so that the positive feedback loop continues.

the listed companies. Financial exchanges are by no means unique in following this strategy.

The LSE and other exchanges, like fish markets and online meeting places, offer a critical lesson:

THE LESSON

To identify a catalyst community, you should look beyond businesses that exist today; you may have to help create businesses that are needed for the catalytic reaction.

We will see other examples of this lesson later.

Connecting Businesses and People

The contours of a catalyst community are less obvious when we move beyond basic exchanges (buyers and sellers) and matchmakers (men and women). Many innovative catalysts have made their fortunes by connecting businesses and people who didn't seem to have much in common.

Individual merchants, for example, had started letting customers buy now and pay later by the early nineteenth century. If it were evident that one could create value by building a community of many merchants and consumers sharing a common payment device, it wouldn't have taken until almost 150 years later for someone to figure this out.

Diners Club ignited the modern payment card industry by recognizing that cash and checks were inconvenient for merchants and consumers and then discovering groups that it could bring together. It started with a small community at first—restaurants and gourmands in Manhattan. It quickly expanded its vision to serve the much larger travel and entertainment community—restaurants, nightclubs, and hotels, and their patrons—around the world.

Followers such as American Express spread to an even larger community of merchants, eventually including supermarkets and their customers. The growth of the payment card industry has been driven by the continual search for more types of businesses and consumers to put together. Gasoline stations reduced waiting lines, and were able to handle more customers, when they let drivers charge their gasoline at the pump. Home shopping networks such as QVC in the United States have made impulse buying easy through the use of payment cards. The Hong Kong subway system works more smoothly because people can pay quickly for their rides by waving contactless payment cards issued by the Octopus payment system as they enter.

The invention of the general-purpose payment card provides an important lesson for would-be catalysts:

THE LESSON

To identify a catalyst community, start by isolating a problem that businesses or people encounter as a result of high transaction costs. Then look for ways to lower those transaction costs by getting both sides of the transaction on the same platform. This isn't the only way to find a catalyst community, but it has been an important one.

Creating Complementors

Finding and nurturing firms that produce complements, called *complementors,* is the key to the success of many catalyst communities.[8]

A complement is a product that makes another product more valuable. Complements are important in one-sided as well as multisided industries. Firms like Netflix, Inc. or Blockbuster that rent DVDs make DVD players manufactured by firms like Sony more valuable, for instance. Many one-sided businesses make their own complements. Gillette produces shaving cream as well as razors.

Software platform vendors discovered the importance of complements early in their history. Apple computer sales took off after VisiCalc—the first spreadsheet application—was introduced. VisiCalc was one of the first *killer apps*—an application that consumers like so much that it makes them buy a computer device just to get it. Apple didn't do anything to encourage VisiCalc. But the pioneering computer company quickly realized that encouraging the development of more applications—killer or not—would help sell Apples. Guy Kawasaki, Apple's evangelist, encouraged hardware and software makers to create complements for the new computers. Other important killer apps for catalysts are listed in table 3-1.

Ever since spreadsheets ignited the personal computer revolution, software platforms have chosen to treat complementors as customers. Much of the code in a software platform is written to make it easier for complementors to write applications. Evangelists—a real job title at companies such as Google—work at persuading application developers to join the congregation, as we discussed in chapter 2. The result is a sophisticated exercise in building and ultimately reinforcing a catalyst community.

To create a catalyst community, entrepreneurs may find that they have to either encourage the creation of complementors that can become part of the community or provide a set of complements themselves. Palm took the do-it-yourself approach with its introduction of the Palm Pilot—the product that set off a catalytic reaction for personal digital assistants (PDAs). Without a proven track record, Palm didn't think that it could get application developers—the key complementors—to write for it. So it initially produced all the organizer applications itself. Once successful, it had no trouble getting others to write apps. Those applications helped attract new members of the community who were intrigued by a specific application even if they weren't initially interested in the Palm Pilot.

TABLE 3-1

Killer apps outside the computer business

Killer applications aren't just for computers. They are products produced by one part of the catalyst community that ignite a catalytic reaction because they are immensely valuable to another part of the catalyst community. Here are some examples of killer apps outside the computer industry.

The killer app	The catalyst business
Soap opera	Broadcast radio
Foreign trade	Venetian bank notes of exchange
Classified ads	Newspapers
Text messaging	Mobile telephones in Europe
Borrowing	Payment card

NTT DoCoMo also realized it needed to persuade consumers to embrace its new i-mode service (see the box "The Wise Catalyst: The Story of i-mode"). But who would come to a mobile phone–based Web portal with little content? DoCoMo persuaded other companies to establish sixty-seven sites, ranging from mobile banking to games and fortune-telling, well before i-mode was launched. After that, i-mode could appeal to Web site users, who could now access these new applications on their mobile phones.

THE LESSON

To identify a catalyst community, figure out which products will provide valuable complements; then either persuade other businesses to make those products or, if necessary, provide them yourself.

Working with Suppliers

Estée Lauder didn't start a catalyst, but this persistent woman from the Bronx benefited tremendously from a surprising two-sided business. Working with her chemist uncle, she formulated face creams in his kitchen. She tried to persuade department stores to give her counter space to offer her products. She argued that her creams would benefit the stores by generating more traffic. Saks Fifth Avenue finally relented in 1948. The business she founded sold $6.5 billion worth of cosmetics in 2006.[9] In the United States, almost half of its sales are made through department stores and Estée Lauder accounts for half of cosmetic sales made by these department stores.[10]

Although it is less transparent, stores like Saks follow much the same kind of two-sided strategy as a shopping mall. They let shoppers in for free, while charging other merchants for space to sell their own products. Saks gets a commission on what the Estée Lauder Companies, Inc. sells at its cosmetics counters, while the Estée Lauder Companies gets stuck with what doesn't sell. Saks thereby turns the suppliers in the traditional supply chain into partners—members of a community with a shared interest in success. Attracted in part by the Estée Lauder products, the shoppers who come to Saks are part of the community that is built when stores and suppliers cooperate.

The Wise Catalyst: The Story of i-mode

It is said that there are a few things a Japanese teenage girl won't leave home without: her Hello Kitty charm bracelet, Louis Vuitton handbag, pale pink lipstick, and i-mode phone.

I-mode is the mobile phone Internet service launched in Japan in February 1999 by NTT DoCoMo. With more than 50 million subscribers, as of early 2006, it is one of the largest mobile carriers in the world and one of the world's most successful mobile data services.[11] I-mode is most popular among young users, twenty-four to thirty-five years of age, with the heaviest users of i-mode being young women under the age of twenty.

DoCoMo wasn't always such a hot ticket. In fact, it languished for years inside its giant parent company, NTT. Things changed in 1994 when the market for mobile phones in Japan opened up. Inspired by a vision to move beyond voice services, DoCoMo's engineers set off to develop not only the world's smallest mobile phones but a "packet-switched" network that allowed them to easily base charges on the volume of data sent and received rather than on air time.

Now that it had cracked the code on a way to monetize content, DoCoMo set out to assemble the world's first mobile Internet content network. It decided to become a content aggregator, providing two tiers of access: that which could be directly accessed via i-mode's menu bar and that which could be downloaded over the Internet. DoCoMo earned a commission on the content accessed via its menu bar—content that as a result of the

Task 2: Determine How Much Groups Need
Each Other—And Why

Mere attraction isn't enough to make separate groups good candidates for forming a catalyst community. There have to be obstacles to members of one group getting together with members of the

phone's simple user interface was easy to access. It handled all of the billing to subscribers, making it attractive for content owners to sign on to the DoCoMo network.

Subscribers' pricing plans were designed to ignite a catalytic reaction. DoCoMo knew that more subscribers would demand more content, which in turn would bring in more content providers. And they were right.

As of early 2006, there were some 6,000 content providers accessible from i-mode's menu bar and some 94,000 more that were available for access outside of that.[12] Japanese teens keep their handsets on and connected 24/7. Many, accustomed to long daily commutes, use them to catch up on the news, download the latest music, play games with their friends, do their banking, or get the latest sports results.

I-mode's success is a shining example of catalyst wisdom. First, it recognized that its target consumer would be grateful for a technology that gave them something to do on their long commutes. Second, it did not wait until its technology was perfected to roll out its product. It knew that it had a mass market that would prefer to have an adequate but imperfect technology now rather than to wait for a perfect solution some years hence. Third, its pricing strategy proved brilliant. It priced its services so that its customers were not penalized for its technological shortcomings (e.g., slow download speeds) but rather paid for the type of content they wanted. And by offering content owners an efficient way to distribute and bill for content, it was able to attract both the content and the audience.

other group. Catalysts create value by developing ways to lower barriers of this sort.

Not all members of a possible community need a catalyst's help. Many men and women find each other informally and wouldn't think about going to a dating club, much less posting a personal on craigslist. Companies have shown that they can communicate directly with consumers through billboards. Enough members of one group must face hindrances in getting access to enough members of the other for a catalyst to have a viable service.

A successful catalyst entrepreneur must first spot these obstacles and then figure out how to overcome them. To do so, she must develop a thorough understanding of the forces that attract groups to each other. What are the directions of these forces? And how powerful are they? Once she has answers to these questions, she can map out a possible catalyst community, identify the problems that prevent these groups from securing the benefits of attraction, and devise a catalytic solution. (For an example of a catalyst failure see the box "Pets.com: The Poster Child of the Dot-com Collapse.")

Understanding Needs

Buyers and sellers need each other. So do people looking for companionship. Software developers and users do as well. In these and many other cases, there are forces of *mutual attraction*.

Pets.com: The Poster Child of the Dot-com Collapse

Pets.com tried to bring together two groups—pet owners and makers of pet supplies—that were doing just fine with their physical platforms and didn't need a virtual one.

Founded in November 1998, Pets.com followed the business mantra of many of its dot-com counterparts: build a great and memorable brand, and the profits will follow. By December 1999, venture capitalists had invested some $110 million in Pets.com.

Pets.com did what it said it would: it created a memorable brand, including an adorable mascot called the sock puppet, and an attractive and interactive Web site that got more than 1 million hits a day. Its $2 million Super Bowl ad in January 2000 fueled a media frenzy.

Advertisers need viewers, but viewers don't always need advertisers. A study of TiVo found that its users skipped 77 percent of television ads. Another study showed that even those without TiVo took a break 43 percent of the time when commercials played.[13] Of course, while we all complain about ads, most of us find some ads helpful in learning about available products and their prices. Nevertheless, it not too unfair to say that the love that advertisers have for viewers is largely unrequited. There's a *one-directional attraction* between advertisers and viewers much of the time.

The Boston Dispensary showed that *second-degree attractions* sometimes bind portions of a community together. Being human, most doctors were more attracted to the charitable donations than to the impoverished patients. The benefactors provided a link that made the patients valuable to the doctors. Second-degree attractions are common in media businesses. Viewers need content, and this provides the indirect link to advertisers. One-directional and second-degree attractions often go together.

Pets.com, however, failed to follow two fundamental rules of business: know thy customers, and create value for them. Some pet owners might have enjoyed the convenience of ordering pet supplies over the Internet—but not if it was going to cost them more. And while shipping books may be economical for Amazon .com, shipping heavy bags of dog food and kitty litter wasn't for Pets.com. Rather than reducing the transaction costs for pet owners and suppliers, Pets.com increased them.

The only way it could get pet owners on board was to subsidize their purchases. This generated traffic, but it also generated lots of losses. Nearly two years to the day it launched the company, Pets.com shut its doors for good after seeing its stock decline from $11.00 to less than $0.22 in less than eight months.[14]

In the end, Pets.com was a popular brand that wasn't able to create value for pet owners and pet suppliers.

Understanding Wants

Hobo Living would have trouble attracting advertisers or paid subscribers. The forces among the members of the possible catalyst community are weak. By contrast, Jason Binn, founder of Niche Media LLC, discovered strong forces between high society and the businesses that want to sell to its members. *Aspen Peak,* a magazine centered around upscale social life and shopping in Aspen, Colorado, has a limited circulation of about 60,000; most copies are placed in high-end hotel rooms or sent to wealthy households. Advertisers such as Cartier and Chanel fill much of its 250-plus lavish pages. Binn has identified many similar small communities of readers (*Hamptons* and *Ocean Drive* give you the idea) whom certain advertisers find highly attractive. The readers themselves are powerfully attracted to magazines that not only cater to their tastes and advise them about what's "in" and "out" but also feature pictures of many of them at prestigious social gatherings. Moreover, because *Aspen Peak* and publications like it package themselves as an essential guide to elite living, many readers who have never even been to Aspen or the Hamptons enjoy being able to feel as if they are part of these exclusive communities. Table 3-2 lists some other niche magazines.

Stronger attractions provide greater opportunities for creating and capturing value. Members of the catalyst community are willing to pay more for interacting with members to whom they are more powerfully attracted. The catalyst can earn greater profits by setting off and managing a reaction between members who are highly attractive to each other. The lesson for would-be catalysts is:

THE LESSON

Identify groups that are strongly attracted to each other but can't easily get together on their own.

Niche Media capitalized on these strong attractions by focusing on small concentrated communities—communities defined by those who actually live there and those who enjoy following their lifestyle. Many other catalysts find that they can magnify the attractions by building large dispersed communities. No member of

TABLE 3-2

Targeted magazines: their audience and advertisers

Magazine	Audience	Representative advertisers
Cape Cod Life	Residents of Cape Cod, Massachusetts	The Black Cat restaurant Rockland Trust New England Jewelry
Jewelry W	Women who spend $60,000 or more annually on jewelry	Roberto Coin Cartier Judith Ripka Companies, Inc.
Quince Girl	Hispanic girls approaching and planning a *quinceanera*	Tiffany Designs Mori Lee David's Bridal
Asia and Away	25- to 39-year-old English-speaking customers interested in leisure travel to China and the wider Asia region	Sheraton Hotels Intrepid Travel Lan Kwai Entertainment
Decanter	High-end wine lovers	Sutter Home Mercedes Sotheby's
Restaurant Startup & Growth	Americans who dream of opening their own restaurants	Cascades Allen Canning Company Heartland Payment Systems Napa Valley Wines
GRAND	Well-to-do baby boomer grandparents	GlaxoSmithKline The Golf Warehouse Fidelity Investments
All In	Poker enthusiasts	Golden Palace Casino Bubble Insurance World Federation of Poker

a group is strongly attracted to a randomly selected member of another group. But each member of one group has a small probability of being a great match (for trade or companionship) for each member of another group. Larger communities thus increase the expected value each member receives.

A randomly selected American Express cardholder, for example, is unlikely ever to walk in the door of a randomly selected American Express merchant. Yet each cardholder values the security that a certain kind of merchant will probably accept his card for payment, and each merchant recognizes that many of its shoppers will have an American Express card in their wallets.

Prospective catalysts, therefore, need to look beyond the attraction the member of one group has for the member of another group.

THE LESSON

They must also look at the attraction between an individual member of one group and all the members of the other group.

It is hardly remarkable that the absolute magnitude of the forces between members of the catalyst community is something to which an entrepreneur should pay attention. It is less obvious but almost as important that an entrepreneur look at the relative magnitude of these attractions.

The dating scene provides the intuition. A recent study of speed dating found a result that few readers will find surprising. Men look for a lot of dating possibilities.[15] They will seek a real date with any woman they've met at the speed dating exercise who exceeds some modest threshold of attractiveness to them. Women look for just a few good men; they will seek a real date with only a few of the best candidates. Men therefore value having additional women at a dating venue more than women value having additional men. That's one reason women often get a price break at such venues.

Faced with unbalanced forces, entrepreneurs often must devise business models that impose more of the costs of the side that values the other side relatively more, and provide more inducements to the side that values the other side relatively less. We take up the role of unbalanced forces in the next chapter, on catalyst pricing.

Task 3: Look at Who Else Is Serving the Community

When most Europeans pay with plastic, they use debit cards issued by the banks where they have their checking accounts. The credit card is as alien as a peanut butter and jelly sandwich to a French-man. Until the early 1990s, exactly the opposite was true in the United States. Most Americans used credit cards. Few had debit cards because banks didn't issue them and merchants didn't take them. By 2005, however, debit cards accounted for more than 34 percent of the dollar value of card transactions in the United States, and debit card use was growing at three times the rate of credit card use (figure 3-2 shows the growth over time).[16] Two catalytic reactions were behind this.

First, for years many banks had issued ATM cards to their checking account customers and operated ATM machines in their service areas. They belonged to ATM networks in which banks pooled their machines so that their customers could take cash out of any machine owned by any participating bank. ATM networks like X-Press 24 thought that the cardholders would be interested in using these cards to pay for things at merchants; they recognized as well that supermarkets and other merchants that thought credit

FIGURE 3-2

Credit versus debit usage in the United States, 1994–2005

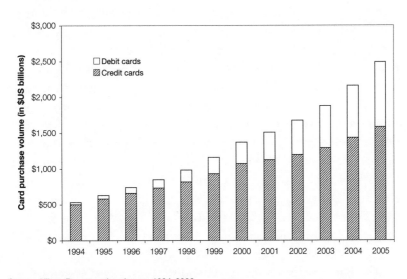

Source: Nilson Report, various issues, 1994–2006

cards were too expensive would be interested in a less expensive way of allowing their customers to pay with plastic. The ATM systems already had the cardholders. They needed to get merchants to take the cards and install PIN pads—card readers that customers could use to enter the personal identification number (PIN) that they used for ATM withdrawals. They got the merchants on board by offering low prices for card transactions, and by 2005 more than 1.6 million merchant locations had PIN pads.[17]

Second, MasterCard and Visa had offered debit cards to their member banks almost from their beginnings. A few banks issued these to their customers, who could then use them at any merchant that accepted the MasterCard or Visa brand. In 1991, however, a quarter century after these card systems started, only 3 percent of their card transactions, measured by dollar value, were on debit cards. Part of the problem was linguistic confusion: people associated debit cards with debt. Another part was that banks didn't see any profit in issuing debit cards. Visa solved the first problem by marketing the debit card as a "check card" that people could use just like a check, and solved the second one by convincing banks that the merchant fees would make the cards worth their while. MasterCard followed suit. By 2005, U.S. banks had issued more than 267 million debit cards—which is what everyone calls them despite the original renaming efforts. Holders can use these at almost any merchant that accepts these card brands; people usually sign for their purchases, so these are called "signature debit cards" in contrast to PIN debit cards, for which people enter a PIN.

The remarkable thing is that these are almost always the same card. The front of your debit card will have a MasterCard or Visa brand on it—telling you that you can use it with a signature at almost any merchant that accepts that brand. The back will have the logo of one or more ATM systems—telling you that you can use it with a PIN at almost any merchant that has a PIN pad. Nowadays many merchants have card readers that give you the choice of using your debit card with a signature or a PIN. As of 2005, signature debit captured 63 percent of debit card volume and PIN debit the remaining 37 percent.[18]

The battle between the ATM and the credit card systems illustrates several lessons for entrepreneurs to consider before embarking on a two-sided business.

THE LESSONS

Identify who else can bring the prospective community together. The ATM systems had cardholders but no merchants, while the credit card systems had merchants but no cardholders. But both were well positioned to bring these groups together. They were necessarily on a collision course.

Assess the business model used by the probable competitors. The ATM and credit card systems used completely opposite pricing schemes to solve opposite problems. The credit card systems needed a revenue stream from merchants to provide banks with incentives to issue cards, while the ATM systems had to offer low prices to merchants to get them to install PIN pads; the banks already had incentives to issue ATM cards because they conserved teller time and provided other valuable services to checking account customers. These competing systems had conflicting business models, like the intersecting catalysts we saw in the previous chapter, even though they were serving the same customer groups.

Identify emerging technologies that could provide a different way to get the groups together. A new firm called Tempo is posing a threat to both debit systems. Many Americans rely on the Automated Clearinghouse House Network (ACH) for direct deposit of payroll checks and for automatic bill payments. Tempo is using the ACH Network for a card that merchants can issue to their customers and thereby save on the fees charged by both signature and PIN debit. Tempo is also a catalyst, but one that might prove more attractive than the existing payment platforms that merchants use.

Looking at the competition is hardly a new concept. But catalysts face more treacherous waters than other start-ups. Many have foundered because their paying customers could get the same product for less from another catalyst with a different business model.

Task 4: Compare Multisided with
One-Sided Business Models

Just because it is possible to create a catalyst to provide an innovative product or service doesn't mean that a catalyst is the only business model or even the best one. The Boston physicians might have gotten the Commonwealth of Massachusetts to provide funding for the dispensary. Then the dispensary could have hired doctors as full-time employees and offered subsidized medical services to the poor. Entrepreneurs and their investors need to consider alternatives for their businesses and make sure that building a catalyst is the best way to create and capture value.

As of 2006, the Apple iPod/iTunes music business is a runaway hit. Apple has sold more than 58 million iPods and more than 1 billion tunes.[19] Figure 3-3 shows iPod's rapid growth since its launch. Apple's market capitalization had increased, as of August 2006, more than 900 percent since the iPod was introduced in October 2001, compared with about 42 percent for the NASDAQ overall and –6 percent for its archrival, Microsoft.[20]

Most of Apple's competitors are based on software platforms that anchor a community of hardware makers, music stores, and content providers. Thus far Apple has decided on a single-sided business model in which it controls the entire supply chain.[21] It licenses the music from content providers, sells it on its online store, and provides a music device that plays only songs from iTunes. It benefits from tight integration.

Microsoft banked on the power of a catalytic reaction. The software giant worked with hardware partners such as Rio and Virgin Electronics that sold portable music players that relied on its media software platform. It also had its own music download service on MSN. After being trounced by the single-sided iPod model, Microsoft decided to introduce its own integrated system called Zune, which includes the portable music player, the software platform that runs it, and a download service. Zune was announced in September 2006 to mixed reviews.

FIGURE 3-3

Sales of iPods and iTunes songs

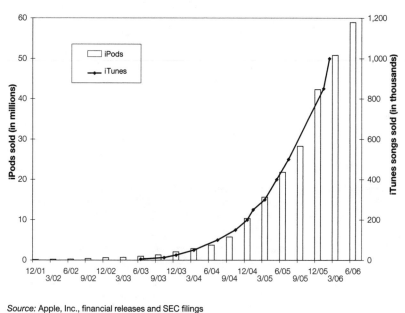

Source: Apple, Inc., financial releases and SEC filings

For now, though, the lesson is:

THE LESSON

Compare the best two-sided strategy with the best single-sided strategy and evaluate whether the benefits of tight integration and control from being a single-sided business outweigh the benefits of positive feedback and flexibility from being a multisided business.

Sometimes entrepreneurs start single-sided businesses with the intent to evolve them into catalysts over time; table 3-3 summarizes some key examples. As we noted earlier, that's what Palm did. It wanted to make sure that it got the hardware and software just right to establish itself. Once it did that, it figured it could make a

TABLE 3-3

The move from one to two sides

BBC	Viewers of the BBC's public service station in the United Kingdom pay via a tax on their televisions. Their commercial services stations outside the United Kingdom sell advertising, which helps keep the tax low.
Sirius Satellite Radio	Listeners paid subscription fees for advertising-free music channels. Sirius added advertising-supported news and sports channels.
TiVo	Subscribers paid for a service that allowed them to download television shows without the commercials. TiVo added services that allowed advertisers to insert infomercials and other long-form advertisements that consumers could opt to play.
Munsey's Magazine	Like many American magazines in the nineteenth century, *Munsey's Magazine* was entirely financed through subscription fees. Then, in 1893, Munsey started inserting advertising.
Atari	Atari originally made its own games. After Space Invaders showed the value of third-party games, Atari began courting third-party games for its game console.

Sources: In the BBC example, U.K. residents must pay a television licensing fee, which supports the BBC's public service broadcasting. In return, the BBC is not permitted to carry advertising or sponsorship on its public service stations in the United Kingdom. The BBC does run commercial television services around the world, which also generate profit in order to keep the license fee low in the United Kingdom. See "Advertising," About the BBC page, BBC Web site, http://www.bbc.co.uk/info/policies/advertising.shtml.

In the Atari example, the company licensed Space Invaders from Japan's Taito. See Peter J. Coughlan and Debbie Freier, "Competitive Dynamics in Home Video Games (A): The Age of Atari," Case 9-701-091 (Boston: Harvard Business School, 2001).

persuasive case to application developers. This tactic worked: one year after it introduced the Pilot, it had two thousand software developers writing for its operating system, and in 2005, the Palm OS ran on hardware made by more than thirteen firms.[22] (Microsoft might have the same strategy in mind for Zune. Time will tell.)

THE LESSON

Consider starting as a single-sided business where all aspects of the ecosystem can be controlled and then creating a two-sided business after establishing the market.

Platform Communities and the
Catalyst Framework

Much value creation in the economy involves either trade, in its many forms, or companionship. Making those interactions among everyone who participates in the society—people, businesses, non-profits, and other entities—more plentiful and more efficient is the job of the catalyst. And over the history of mankind, it has become clear that entrepreneurs are always discovering new ways of helping members of society get together and create value.

So if you are an aspiring catalyst, you don't need to worry that there is nothing left for you to do. You do, though, have to figure out some new source of value that can be created by bringing people together, just as the founders of the Boston Dispensary did, or a more efficient way to bringing members of society together, as

TABLE 3-4

Identifying the platform community

Tasks	Lessons
Identify distinct groups that need each other.	• Think beyond today: look for an underserved group that would benefit from being brought together. • Look for ways to reduce the costs to each group of finding the other. • Identify complements and devise a plan for providing those products or services.
Determine how much groups need each other—and why.	• Identify groups that are strongly attracted to each other but cannot easily get together on their own.
Look at who else is serving the community.	• Determine who else is serving the proposed catalyst community and evaluate their business models for doing so.
Make sure that a multi-sided business model is better than a single-sided one.	• Compare the benefits of integration and control from a single-sided business with the benefits of positive feedback and flexibility from a two-sided business.

craigslist has done for those who used to list in and buy from the newspaper classifieds. In figuring out the new source of value, or the new source of efficiency, you will necessarily have to scope out the catalyst community—the groups whose members will benefit from interacting, in the ways you have identified, with members of other groups. Table 3-4 summarizes the tasks involved.

Pricing is also central to creating and capturing value for a catalyst. We turn to this next.

4

Establish a Pricing Structure

They don't take eyeballs at the bank.

—JIM CRAMER

LOLA, THE FOUNDER OF MAGPOWER, HAS SPENT THE LAST four years creating a powerful new technology that makes multiple computing devices work better.[1] For it to work, consumers must have an X-Mag, and manufacturers must equip their computing devices with a Y-Mag. Consumers who hear what an X-Mag will do if computing devices are equipped with Y-Mags all have the same reaction: "Wow! That would be fantastic."

Companies that make computing devices (like iPods) and companies that rely on those devices (as mobile operators rely on mobile phones) are also excited about the technology, but they have two reservations. It costs something to equip their devices with the Y-Mag. And only consumers who have access to an X-Mag will value this feature.

Many traditional business analysts would say that Lola faces the familiar chicken-and-egg problem: which comes first—the consumers with the X-Mags or the manufacturers with the Y-Mags? Framing the business challenge this way suggests that she must get one side signed up before the other side. That might lead her to despair. It could also take her down an analytical dead end as she tries to figure out how to sign up device makers with nary a consumer in sight. In fact, many successful catalysts figure out how to get both sides on board their platforms at about the same time. Auctions get both buyers and sellers to show up before the first gong rings, and card systems had merchants and cardholders signed up before the first card was used to buy dinner. Instead of pondering which came first, the chicken or the egg, they figured out, so to speak, how to get the hens and roosters together and encourage them to make a lot of baby chicks.

MagPower's challenge is to find value propositions for consumers and device makers that persuade both groups of customers to show up at the party more or less at the same time. Pricing is one key to that. Some catalysts have found that they can start a profitable reaction by charging—and earning profits from—both sides. Others have found that they can start a reaction only by pricing low—perhaps at cost, possibly even lower—to one side. MagPower must search for those golden prices that set off the reaction and also result in the most profits possible. This is the main objective of element 2 of the catalyst framework.

To pursue this objective, Lola and other aspiring catalyst entrepreneurs must explore several issues to find the prices that lead to a successful *and* profitable catalytic reaction. We've identified five critical tasks entrepreneurs must perform to complete the pricing element of the catalyst framework, shown in figure 4-1.

1. **Set separate prices for access and usage.** What kinds of prices should a catalyst consider? Most catalysts can consider charging customers for gaining admission to a physical or virtual platform and for using the platform to interact with other customers. After careful thought, of course, they may decide that some of these prices should be zero—or even negative.

2. **Set prices to balance the demand from two sides.** What prices will get the best mix of customers to participate in

FIGURE 4-1

The catalyst framework: establish a pricing structure

Identify the platform community	Establish a pricing structure	Design the catalyst for success	Focus on profitability	Compete strategically with other catalysts	Experiment and evolve
• Identify distinct groups that need each other	• Set separate prices for access and usage	• Attract multiple customer groups that need each other	• Study industry history	• Understand the dynamics of catalyst competition	• Know when to be first— and when to follow
• Determine why and how much they need each other	• Set prices to balance demand from two sides	• Promote interactions	• Use forecasts to enhance profitability	• Look for competition from different business models	• Control growth
• Evaluate who else is serving the community	• Price to grow slowly— at first	• Minimize transaction costs	• Anticipate competitor actions	• Leverage to attack	• Protect your back
• Compare a multisided business model with a single-sided one	• Pay customers to belong— sometimes	• Design for evolution	• Align interests internally and externally	• Consider cooperation	• Plan for what's next
	• Price for long-term profits				• Look out for the cops
Find out who needs whom— and why	**Shape participation and maximize profits**	**Draw customers and facilitate interactions**	**Visualize path toward long-term profit**	**Challenge existing catalysts and react to new catalyst threats**	**Pursue evolutionary strategy for growth**

the catalytic reaction? Most catalysts have the same problem as a dating club: if they don't get the right balance from the groups they serve, they won't have a business.

3. **Price to grow slowly—at first.** What prices will ignite the catalytic reaction and provide for controlled growth? Many successful catalysts have started small and expanded slowly by finding prices that capture and promote the forces that flow between members of the catalyst community. Many failed catalysts have fallen into to the trap of trying to get too big too quickly.

4. **Pay customers to belong (sometimes).** When should a catalyst subsidize a group of customers? Lots of successful

catalysts don't make profits from at least one significant
group of customers. But by getting these customers to participate in the catalytic reaction, they make more than
enough profits from another group of customers to offset
their losses. Of course, countless catalysts have gone bankrupt giving too much away.

5. **Price for long-term profits.** What prices will lead to long-
term profitability? Igniting a catalytic reaction and harnessing its forces does not guarantee that a catalyst will
ever see positive earnings, much less earn a fortune. Many
catalysts make significant investments in creating a virtual
or physical platform, and getting an adequate return on
that capital isn't easy. That is why catalysts must evaluate
whether the best prices are in fact good enough to sustain a
profitable long-term reaction.

There is one vital omission from this list: price with an eye to the
competition. The topic of competition with and between catalysts is
quite complex, however, and it goes well beyond pricing, so we de-
vote an entire chapter to it. We now turn to examine each of the five
tasks listed earlier—and the questions they raise about pricing.

Task 1: Set Separate Prices for Access and Usage

Catalysts typically have a complex array of potential pricing strategies. At the simplest level, they can charge different prices to each
group of customers they serve. Condé Nast charges readers $4.95
for a copy of *Vogue* magazine at the newsstand and charges advertisers more than twenty thousand times that for a full-page color ad
each month.

Moreover, in principle at least, many catalysts can also charge
members of each group one price for getting *access* to the physical or
virtual platform they have created and another price depending on
how much they *use* that platform for interactions. American Express, to take one example, charges cardholders a $2,500 member-
ship fee for its ultraexclusive Centurion Card. It doesn't charge them

anything for using the card; in fact, it lavishes cardholders with rewards and other perks based on use—a negative usage fee. On the other side of the market, merchants don't have to pay a membership fee to take these cards. But whenever the merchant and cardholder place a transaction on this card, the merchant pays about 2.6 percent of the amount of the transaction to American Express.[2]

Filling out the pricing matrix shown in table 4-1 is an important task for catalysts. In each case, the entry could be positive (customers pay), negative (customers get a perk), or zero (customers don't pay anything but don't get any extra incentives, either).

Before we explain how separate fees for access and usage can help guide catalysts toward long-term profitability, we provide an overview of the pricing schemes that a few successful catalysts have adopted.

Residential real estate agents in many cities and towns in the United States operate multiple listing services that facilitate buyers and sellers meeting each other. Sellers generally pay a 6 percent commission if their property sells. Buyers pay nothing. And neither prospective buyers nor sellers pay anything to gain access to the multiple listing services or the help of the agents who use them. So there is a 6 percent usage fee for one side; the other three possible prices are zero.

Video game console makers provide software and hardware platforms. Sony PlayStation and Microsoft Xbox are the two leaders. Independent game developers such as Electronic Arts write games for these platforms. Consumers buy the consoles from the platform makers and the games from the developers (as well as the platform makers). Sony and Microsoft have roughly the same pricing scheme. They charge game developers an access fee for the

TABLE 4-1

The catalyst pricing matrix (the case of credit cards)

	Side 1 (merchants)	Side 2 (cardholders)
Access	0 (minimal fees to join)	+ (annual membership fees)
Usage	+ (per-transaction charges)	– (float and reward fees)

technical information required to write games and a usage fee that could amount to roughly 30 percent of a game title's price.[3] They sell consoles to consumers at an access fee that is usually at or below manufacturing cost. Consumers pay no usage fee.

The difference between access and usage fees isn't always apparent. To take one example, companies pay about $560,000 for a thirty-second spot on the popular American television series *Desperate Housewives*.[4] That sounds like an access fee. In fact, that price is based on the usual number and types of people who watch the show and are therefore likely to see the advertisement. If the rating services report a decline in viewers, the network will ordinarily give the advertiser some money back or an advertising credit. Generally, media companies charge advertisers prices that are best characterized as usage fees because they depend on the number of viewers, which is an estimate of the number of possible interactions with viewers.

Access and usage fees help accomplish different objectives for setting off and fueling a catalytic reaction.

Access fees are particularly helpful for making sure the catalyst has enough of the right kind of customers on each side. A low admission fee will encourage customers to sign up and try a two-sided business. That is especially important for getting a catalytic reaction going. Customers on one side may not be sure about how much value they will get from interacting with any of the customers on the other side. If it is cheap to join, they may try and see. That is a reason video game console companies have kept console prices cheap. They want consumers to buy the consoles and try the games. Keeping admission fees high makes sense for other catalysts. It may help get the "right" customers to join the community—and simultaneously discourage the "wrong" kind of customers. That's what the $55,000 entry fee did for the movers and shakers club mentioned in the last chapter.

Usage fees are important for guiding the catalytic reaction. Low ones encourage customers to intermingle. That's what most catalysts adopt for at least one side. Most exchanges charge buyers or sellers only if they complete a transaction. Participants generally don't pay for making or considering a bid. Readers and viewers don't pay according to how much content they consume; as mentioned earlier, advertising fees track the number of eyeballs, though (and in Internet venues, the number of click-throughs). Of course, the two-drink minimum, paid as part of admission (an access fee), facilitates mingling at many bars. Table 4-2 summarizes the purposes of access and usage fees.

Low usage fees make particular sense for the customer side that is most likely to initiate the interaction. Cardholders decide when to use a card to pay for goods and services. Credit card issuers have therefore given cardholders free float, reward miles, and other benefits that increase with the value of purchases.

The lesson for catalysts:

THE LESSON

Set separate prices for access and usage to encourage customers to join and use the platform. Charge low prices to the customers you need most for a catalytic reaction.

TABLE 4-2

Access versus usage fees

Access fees	Usage fees
Objective: to control access to the physical or virtual platform	*Objective: to control use of the platform's services in order to interact with customer groups*
Ensure that the catalyst has enough of the right kind of customers on each side	Guide the catalytic reaction
Low admission fees encourage customers to sign up and to get the catalytic reaction going	Low usage fees encourage customers to interact
High admission fees help get the "right" customers to join the community	High usage fees inhibit participation of the customer side most likely to initiate the interaction
Example: video game consoles are cheap because they encourage customers to buy consoles; in turn, customers buy many games	*Example*: credit card issuers offer rewards for using the card and provide free float between the time of the charge and the time of the bill

Task 2: Set Prices to Balance the
Demand from All Sides

Achieving balance between the groups served by the catalyst is also key to finding the prices that maximize long-term profits. There's no point in having one thousand sellers show up at an auction if only a single buyer appears. The auction would create far more value for its participants if there were forty sellers and fifteen buyers. That means raising the price to sellers and lowering it to buyers.

Christie's has found that it gets the right balance by charging both buyers and sellers. Admission to the auctions is free to both. But sellers pay a percentage of the value of what they sell during the year; they are charged on a sliding scale that begins at 20 percent and falls to 2 percent. Buyers pay 20 percent of the first $20,000 they spend and 12 percent on any amount over that.[5] In 2004, this grande dame of auction houses hosted the Eric Clapton Guitar Auction, one of its widely covered "pop culture" auctions. Hundreds of bidders—in person and on the phone—vied for eighty-eight guitars from the world's most famous rock and roll musicians. This eagerly anticipated event, which was done to benefit one of Eric Clapton's favorite charities, raised $7.4 million and fetched the highest price ever paid for a single guitar ($959,500 for Eric Clapton's famous "Blackie" guitar).[6]

The right prices depend on the proper proportions for the catalytic reaction. Just as a chef needs different combinations of ingredients, depending on what he's cooking, catalysts need different combinations of customers, depending on the particulars of their venture.

Advertising-supported media have a special balancing consideration. Readers and viewers won't tolerate too much advertising relative to content. A typical thirty-minute television show in the United States has eight minutes of advertising, for instance. Attempts by some stations to increase that amount have led viewers to switch to other stations, which of course reduces what advertisers will pay. Radio listeners seem particularly prone to switching away from advertising, and popular radio stations in the United

States sometimes differentiate themselves by highlighting that they play fifteen minutes of music uninterrupted by advertising. They must then increase advertising rates to limit demand for space to the amount that viewers will accept.

Software platforms have to balance the number of applications with the number of end users. Almost all have found that the best pricing scheme involves giving away access to the software platform to developers to encourage them to write applications and charging end users for access to the software platform. Symbian, for example, charges phone manufacturers $7.25 to license each copy of its operating system ($5.00 after the first 2 million are sold), and those manufacturers pass that cost along so that it is ultimately borne by phone buyers.[7] But it makes software code available to developers for free and, like other platform vendors, offers tools that help developers use its software code at modest prices. As of mid-2006, 82.8 million people used Symbian-powered mobile phones and had more than 6,700 applications available to them.[8]

THE LESSON

Set access and usage fees to balance the demand from the two sides—to make sure there are enough customers on each side to provide value to customers on the other side.

Task 3: Price to Grow Slowly—at First

A catalytic reaction starts only when enough customers from both sides are brought together. An important finding of our research is that enough is often not very many. Successful two-sided businesses often start out with a small number of customers from each side—small, that is, relative to the customers they obtain a year or five years later. The Fox network, for example, began in 1986 with a one-hour late-night talk show that aired daily. It attracted a small audience and couldn't charge much for advertising time on that show.

But bringing the two sides together in these modest ways can provide enough value for the participants to get a viable business going and ignite the market. Once other members of the community see this value, they join too, further increasing the value. These continuous feedbacks attract even more members to the community. Not forever, but until the size expands to the natural limits of the physical or virtual platform operated by the catalyst. In this way, Microsoft established a powerful feedback loop with its pricing of Windows. This blockbuster product was first introduced in the middle 1980s at a time when people who used IBM-compatible PCs had to key in commands on a "command line" and the mouse was an Apple-only novelty. Windows 1.0 provided a visual interface—similar to what Apple had introduced for its Lisa computers. Priced then at $100, this trial version of Windows attracted only a few thousand users. Developers could write applications for it for free. At first only a few did.

Microsoft improved Windows substantially through subsequent releases. By 1990, it was set to release Windows 3.0, which had a vast array of new features for consumers and developers. Prices stayed low, though: end users could license Windows 3.0 for less than $150, and computer manufacturers for much less.[9] This was considered reasonable since applications for the PC were often going for much more, other operating systems were much more costly, and developers continued to get access to valuable services for free. The value proposition attracted both developers and consumers. The catalytic reaction that was ignited in 1985 exploded in 1990. Five years later, in 1995, Windows had 100 million users who had more than 28,000 applications available to them.[10]

Of course, the design and features included in Windows were important to its success. But pricing was also critical. Had Microsoft charged more for Windows, consumers would have been less interested in it—especially when it was new and unproven. Software developers then wouldn't have written applications using it, no matter how good its services were. Without enough consumers, they wouldn't make money selling their application programs. If Microsoft had tried to charge developers, it would have discouraged them from writing the applications that were necessary to attract consumers at all.

As with most catalysts, this strategy seems obvious after the fact. That it wasn't obvious at the time can be seen from the strategy that IBM, a highly sophisticated and experienced computer hardware and software maker, followed for its own OS/2, which competed with Windows. IBM set OS/2's end-user price at twice that of Windows. When OS/2 was released in 1987, there were few useful applications for it. IBM hadn't invested enough in getting the developers on board; many feared—correctly, as it turned out—that the high prices would turn away end users, thus limiting the market for any applications the developers might produce. OS/2 limped along with few users and developers through the 1990s and was finally killed off by IBM in 2005.

THE LESSON

Catalysts must price to harness the attractions between customer groups, setting access and usage charges to generate positive feedback effects between the two sides. Better to start small and grow slowly with the right proportions than to start big with the wrong ones.

Task 4: Pay Customers to Belong (Sometimes)

Catalysts often make substantial investments to develop and maintain a virtual or physical platform for the communities they serve. They and their investors reap a return only by securing significant operating profits from at least one customer group. (*Operating profit* refers to the difference between the revenues received from a customer group and the direct cost of serving that group, with no allocations of the costs of developing the catalyst's platform.) They therefore need to consider carefully how the access and usage prices they charge will contribute to profitability.

Figuring out how much operating profit should come from each side is one of the most critical decisions a catalyst makes. It requires calculating the access and usage prices that balance demand, generating positive feedbacks, and generating enough operating income in aggregate to cover development costs and provide a long-run return that compensates for what are often considerable risks.

The best way to accomplish all this is to start with the map of the prospective community that we described in the last chapter. An entrepreneur should then assess how much members of each customer group need members of the other customer groups.

In some cases, the intensity of the needs will be similar. That often makes *symmetric pricing,* in which both customer groups contribute operating profits. Sotheby's and Christie's charge both buyers and sellers and thereby make money from both sides of the auction market. Insurance brokers help companies manage their risks and find insurers that can cover those risks. They often get paid by both the companies and the insurers.[11]

In other cases, the intensities will be dissimilar. One side will need the other side much more. That makes it attractive to use *asymmetric pricing,* in which one customer group gets a significant break. The less interested group needs a boost to join the community since it doesn't value being part of it as much as the other group. Meanwhile, the more interested group often places a high value on the less interested group and is therefore willing to pay a high price. With asymmetric pricing, the preponderance—and maybe even all—of the operating profit comes from the more interested group. That's the case for the yellow pages, which usually obtain all of their revenues from the businesses that list themselves and place advertisements and none from consumers, whom they also serve.

As a matter of fact, our research shows that asymmetric pricing is the norm for catalysts. It apparently doesn't take much of a difference in the intensity of demand for the two sides to lead catalysts to a pricing scheme in which one group contributes little or no operating profit or maybe even gets subsidized. Table 4-3 lists several examples of successful catalysts that subsidize a major part of their community.

In practice, successful catalysts adopt two seemingly different asymmetric pricing strategies to start and maintain the feedbacks. Many set the price to one side of the business so that their revenues just about cover their operating costs. Most readers pay a newsstand or subscription price that roughly covers the cost of printing and distributing the newspaper. Video game console makers sell their boxes at roughly the cost of manufacturing—sometimes a bit above, sometimes a bit below. Although this has varied with the intensity of competition, payment card issuers have often charged

TABLE 4-3

Successful catalysts that subsidize some customers

Company	Service	Subsidized side
Manpower	Matches employers with temporary employees	Employees don't pay for matching
Google	Matches advertisers and customers through Internet-search service	People don't pay for search
News Corporation	Produces and distributes many newspapers	Readers just cover the cost of printing and distribution
Simon Property Group, Inc.	Operates a chain of shopping malls	Shoppers don't pay to get into the malls
Realtor.com	Internet-based multiple listing service	Buyers don't pay for listing access
Gerson Lehrman Group	Consulting firm that matches a company's need for experts with experts who have the right expertise	Experts don't pay for access to the service that matches them to client needs

annual fees that roughly offset the value of the float and other perks they give cardholders.

Other catalysts don't charge customers on one side anything. Suburbanites seldom pay for parking at shopping malls. Software that is free to one group of users is also quite common: you can download Adobe Acrobat for reading PDF files and RealPlayer for listening to music and watching videos. Similarly, job seekers look for positions for free on Monster.com, while employers pay to post their ads. However, in all these cases, the incremental cost of providing the good or service to these customers is quite low given that the good or service is provided at all. Once Adobe has created its software, for example, the additional cost of distributing a copy over the Internet to people who want to read PDFs is trivial. As with the newspaper that just about covers its incremental cost by charging newsstand buyers $1, Adobe just about covers its incremental cost by charging $0.

Optimal pricing requires careful research into the needs of the catalyst community and its sensitivity to prices. However, there are a few general lessons that catalysts can follow:

THE LESSONS

Consider prices that lead to zero or negative operating profits from a customer group that is (a) very valuable to another customer group and (b) does not place a high value on that other customer group.

Consider zero access fees for members of a customer group who are uncertain about the value they will receive from joining. Also consider subsidizing membership for a customer group that is highly desired by another customer group.

Consider zero (or even negative) usage fees for members of a customer group who either initiate an interaction with the other customer group or are highly valuable to the other customer group.

It is possible that as the catalyst community expands, the business will find that it is profitable to modify these prices. Yahoo! Auctions didn't charge sellers anything when it started its online auction site in Japan. Only when it achieved a critical mass of customers did it add monthly access fees. Finally, it charged sellers commissions (usage fees) after its success was ensured and it felt it could weather any potential fallout to a competitor.

Our research has revealed, however, that most industries with catalysts are born with a price structure—one that determines the extent to which operating profits come from one side or the other—and that, like having blue eyes, this price structure remains a feature of the industry throughout its life.[12] The merchant-pays model for payment cards, for example, has remained the dominant approach in the United States and most other countries ever since it was pioneered in 1950. Likewise, consumers haven't paid to get into or use shopping malls since they became popular in the 1960s in the United States. That's true in all countries with which we are familiar.

Should MagPower, the company we described at the outset of this chapter, seek its operating profit from both sides, only from consumers, or only from device makers? Should it subsidize one of these sides—by, for example, selling X-Mag to consumers at less than manufacturing cost or paying device makers a small fee for incorporating Y-Mag into their products? In general, catalysts should give the price break to the side that is needed the most for the reaction. Careful review of MagPower shows that to get this technology off the ground, the company needs the device makers much more than the consumers. Remember, consumers say, "Wow!" but the device makers only say, "Sounds great, but . . ." So the price break goes to the device makers.

That still leaves the question of how much of a break. Initially, MagPower may find that it has to provide a royalty-free license, or even some small inducements, to get device makers to include the Y-Mag feature. Then it can charge consumers for the X-Mag products that work with the Y-Mag features. At this point, the search for the best prices becomes somewhat simpler. Once MagPower has fixed the price for device makers (perhaps a zero royalty), it can focus on the best price for consumers, keeping in mind that the more it charges consumers, the fewer consumers it will get on board. The fewer consumers it gets on board, the fewer device manufacturers will get on board even at a zero royalty. And the fewer device manufacturers it gets, the more resistant consumers will be to pay for the X-Mag.

That is not to say that Lola should also give X-Mag away to consumers—that would lead to bankruptcy. But it is to say that she needs to consider the feedback effects between the two sides in setting the price. Of course, as with new products in traditional industries, it may make sense to give the product away during an introductory period, to one or both sides, just to give some customers experience with the product. These prices could then be raised to one or both sides after the product has gained traction in the marketplace.

As she readies the launch of MagPower, it would be natural for Lola to set up two divisions. The X-Division would be responsible for selling X-Mags to consumers. The Y-Division would be in charge of getting Y-Mags in the hands of device makers. Many companies would give divisions like these separate P&Ls and compensate the division heads in large part based on their financial performance. And that's what several two-sided businesses we encountered in our research did. All came to rue the day they took this traditional approach.

The problem is obvious in hindsight. Let's suppose for Mag-Power to succeed, it has to charge device makers a nominal fee and

TABLE 4-4

Pricing checklist

Price to zero or negative operating profit	Zero membership fees	Zero or negative usage fees
To engage a customer group that is very valuable to another customer group . . .	To engage members of a customer group who are uncertain about the value they will get from joining	To encourage members of a group to interact with another group that values those interactions highly
and does not place a high value on that other customer group	To engage customers who are highly desired by the other customer group but who don't value that other group enough to sign up without some inducement	To persuade members of a group to interact with members of another group even though they don't value those interactions much

make its profits on the consumer side. The Y-Division head will argue against that. He'll have a dismal P&L and fear getting only a pitiful bonus. Misalignment of internal incentives will make it hard for MagPower to find the golden pair of prices. We will return to this difficult issue in chapter 6, but the key lesson to keep in mind is simple:

THE LESSON

You can't divide a two-sided business and evaluate each side by its stand-alone profitability; the two-sided strategy should drive organization and incentives.

Table 4-4 provides a short checklist of pricing considerations.

Task 5: Price for Long-Term Profits

Like any business, a catalyst should closely watch today's bottom line with one eye and scan the long-run profit horizon with the other. Two characteristics of catalysts make the quest for profits more treacherous for two-sided than for single-sided businesses, however: giving things away for a living and walking a tightrope.

As we've seen, many, if not most, catalysts find that they have to just break even or lose money on one side of the business. Not just to break into the market, but forever. It is rare for a single-sided business to decide to lose money on one of its products except for short-term "specials." It is common for catalysts. Unfortunately, any business that gives things away to customers is always a step away from a financial precipice (see the box "The Catalyst Pricing Mountains").

Thousands of entrepreneurs learned this the hard way during the dot-com bust. In what was almost mass hysteria, they seemed to take the old joke about selling each unit at a loss but making it up on volume as a strategic principle. Many followed the advice of Internet gurus that whoever attracted the most users would have the most valuable business—whether it was a Web portal for catering to cat lovers or an auction site for businesses selling to biotechnology firms.

The Catalyst Pricing Mountains

Every business searches for the pricing that maximizes its profits. Whether it is using trial and error or analytical methods, this quest is more arduous and treacherous for two-sided than for one-sided business.

For a single-sided business, looking for the best price is like climbing a simple two-dimensional mountain. Even when the peak is shrouded in clouds, you have some sense of whether you are climbing higher or lower. Moreover, economics has provided some navigational tools that are widely taught in business schools and often used by sophisticated marketers.

For a two-sided business, looking for the best prices is like climbing a complex three-dimensional mountain. The mountain has canyons and precipices. It may also have multiple peaks—you may think that you have climbed to the top, only to have other towering peaks hidden in the clouds. The one-sided navigational tools don't work in large part because they don't account for the interdependencies between the two groups of customers.

Moreover, they believed that whoever grew most quickly would dominate, even though it was never clear why, for instance, selling more cat food would make your Web site more attractive to unaffiliated cat lovers.

Sometimes, however, a dot-com bust was the result of poor catalyst pricing, not just a fuzzy concept. Iwix.net, an online insurance business, had good reason to feel confident about catalyst economics. After all, insurers who are willing to underwrite the losses from a risk in return for a periodic fee and businesses with risks that they would like to insure have been meeting on organized exchanges for millennia. The oldest known one was established in ancient Athens. Lloyds of London, perhaps the most famous group of insurance underwriters, emerged in the late seventeenth century to help bring together those offering and seeking insurance. Iwix.net tried to bring this same concept to the Internet. It focused on specialty insurance—that is, it excluded routine business risks such as fires and theft—and provided a platform for buyers, sellers, and various intermediaries to come together. A big problem, though, according to its former CEO, was "getting people to use the site in volume—and getting them to pay for the convenience of meeting on line."[13] Iwix.net only received revenue for fees on completed transactions, but that wasn't enough to pay the bills. A likely problem with this and other failed specialty insurance exchanges is that the Web is very suited to straightforward matching of buyers and sellers through auctions and other devices. Specialty insurance contracts, however, are complex, and the best match often requires many details that it would appear are better negotiated in person than over the Web.

The lesson for catalysts:

THE LESSON

Make sure that there is a value proposition for all parts of your community and that there are sufficient operating profits from at least one side to deliver a healthy return on investment.

The balancing act—keeping both sides on board and interacting with each other—is the other major source of danger for catalysts. Small deviations from the optimal prices can send a catalyst into an abyss. Raising prices to one group of customers may reduce their participation so much that the other group of customers also stops coming. This can lead to a death spiral as positive feedback effects work in reverse. Single-sided businesses, in contrast, can often raise or lower prices by modest amounts without drastic consequences.

Like many B2Bs, for a time M-Xchange thought it had a great business model. It wanted to help suppliers owned by members of racial and ethnic minorities get business from *Fortune* 1000 companies. Many of these large companies were trying to encourage the use of minority suppliers. M-Xchange planned to charge the minority suppliers 1–2.5 percent of the value of the contracts they secured. It didn't attract enough participants at those prices, however, and intense competition quickly drove the fee down to 0.25 percent. It closed down four months after it went live.[14]

Slate, the first online magazine, pulled itself out of a spiral by quickly retreating. It started out free for readers and began attracting some paid advertising. Then it raised its access fee in March 1998. Monthly visitors plunged from five hundred thousand to two hundred thousand. That made it less attractive to advertisers. It abandoned reader charges a year later. It quickly regained its readers and reached a million monthly visitors in June 1999. At that point, the high readership started luring advertisers. Although it is unclear whether *Slate* could have survived without Microsoft's backing, it was sold in late 2004 for undisclosed "millions" to the *Washington Post*.[15] As of late 2006, it remains free to readers and attracts significant advertising.

Pricing and the Catalyst Framework

MobiTV got its pricing right and, as a result, laid the groundwork for a successful catalyst. As of mid-2006, more than a million people around the world were paying more than $10 a month to watch its television service on mobile phones.[16] When it started in 1999, it had to figure out how to get mobile operators such as Vodafone to offer its service, television networks such as NBC to provide content for it, and subscribers to sign up for it. To do this, it had to get the prices right so that each of these members of its community had a value proposition that got them to sign on. And it had to get a critical mass of content, operators, and subscribers to make any group interested in its service.

MobiTV decided not to create a pricing model out of thin air but to follow a time-tested model—the one that cable television networks had successfully adopted. The television channels and the mobile operators each received a portion of the subscription fee. MobiTV makes its profit from the portion of the subscription fee that is left over. In addition, the television channels permit MobiTV to replace a certain number of the advertisements included in their broadcasts with spots for advertisers that MobiTV signs up—this follows traditional practice in the U.S. cable television business.

Even with this pricing model, MobiTV wasn't able to get the chicken-and-egg sequence right. It faced a common catalyst problem. The mobile operators didn't want to sign on unless they knew that MobiTV was going to be able to offer significant television content for their subscribers. The television channels didn't want to bother until they knew that MobiTV could actually guarantee distribution. In addition, none of them wanted to be first to sign on with a pioneering service that could turn out to be an embarrassing failure. MobiTV used "contingent contracts" to set the stage for a catalytic reaction. Sprint agreed to offer the service if MobiTV obtained a certain number of distribution agreements with television channels. MSNBC and other television channels agreed to make their broadcasts available if Sprint signed on and if other channels signed on. With these contingent contracts in hand, MobiTV got Sprint to agree, and the channels quickly followed. Paul Scanlon, who founded MobiTV, reports that eleven more channels signed their contracts the evening before the launch.

Table 4-5 summarizes what the catalyst must do to establish a pricing structure. There is no universal formula available for all catalysts to use in their pricing decisions. A lot depends on the kind of business the catalyst is in and, as we discuss in chapter 7, the competition it faces. Advertising-supported media have different pricing rules than transaction systems. But this much is certain: getting prices right is critical to building the community and getting members to interact.

TABLE 4-5

Establishing a pricing structure

Tasks	Lessons
Set separate prices for access and use.	• Set separate prices to encourage customers to join and use the platform. • Charge low prices to the customers you need most for a catalytic reaction.
Set prices to balance the demand from two sides.	• Make sure there are enough customers on each side to provide value to customers on the other side.
Price to grow slowly—at first.	• Price to generate positive feedback effects between the two sides. • Start small and grow slowly.
Pay customers to belong (sometimes).	• Prepare to charge one side nothing or even offer "negative usage fees."
Price for long-term profitability.	• Ensure that operating profits come from at least one side of the platform.

Equally important, though, is designing the product so that it appeals to multiple groups and fosters their interaction. MobiTV, for example, developed a convenient graphical user interface for using its television service on mobile phones and obtained channels that appealed to a wide range of subscribers. The product was attractive to multiple communities, which created the opportunity for a catalyst platform.

We turn to product design, the next basic element in the catalyst framework, in the next chapter.

5

Design the Catalyst for Success

Good design is good business.

—Thomas J. Watson

Occupying 11.6 hectares (28.7 acres) in the middle of downtown Tokyo, Roppongi Hills is one of the most exclusive places to live or work in Japan. It has a plethora of upscale shops, many of the best restaurants in the city, and a lively nightlife with packed bars and clubs. The privileged few who both live and work there enjoy one of the most precious commodities in this congested metropolis: a short commute. Meanwhile, the many visitors, both locals and tourists, enjoy the vibrant community made possible by Roppongi's commercial and residential facilities.

Unlike in most other fashionable urban enclaves, almost every aspect of this one was planned. Building tycoon Minoru Mori created Roppongi Hills from four hundred parcels of land he bought over seventeen years. After completing these acquisitions, he built a "city within a city" anchored by the fifty-four-story Mori Tower. Surrounding the tower are smaller buildings, a performance arena, gardens, and walkways. He selected restaurants, shops, and movie theatres to provide the right mix and quality for this neighborhood. The high-priced offices and residences attracted Tokyo's elite. Goldman Sachs occupies ten premium floors of the tower, and many of its wealthy investment bankers live nearby. Such well-heeled workers and residents got the attention of high-priced shops and restaurants.

Mori managed the forces of mutual attraction among the homeowners, corporations, shops, and restaurants so well that Roppongi Hills became a thriving neighborhood almost immediately after it opened its doors in April 2003. A casual observer of the neighborhood might assume that Roppongi Hills was a product of good timing in what has always been a fluctuating Tokyo real estate market. Yet our study of its development reveals that Roppongi Hills is a product of meticulous planning and design. By *design* we do not mean simply its impressive architecture. Instead, we refer to the remarkable interaction of its buildings, its residents, its shop owners, its office space, and its retail spaces that create a catalytic reaction in downtown Tokyo. Mori was not merely lucky. He was able to capitalize on his experience in building shopping malls and office complexes throughout Asia. With Roppongi Hills, Mori shows us how important "product design" is in the catalyst framework—even when the product in question is a thriving urban neighborhood. Fortunately, catalyst entrepreneurs in many other businesses can learn from him. As we will see in this chapter, Mori performed a set of design tasks, summarized in figure 5-1, that are critical for all catalysts:

1. **Attract multiple customer groups that need each other.** After dark, the streets around many city high-rises are deserted. The sleek office buildings of downtown Los Angeles are fine for working hours, but not enough people remain after hours to support the shops and restaurants that could breathe life into the neighborhood. Mori made sure that Roppongi had the right mix of office space and living quarters that would make it hum around the clock from the day it opened.

2. **Promote interactions.** Just getting workers and residents to locate in the same place isn't enough. To create a neighborhood, people and businesses have to interact. Physical de-

FIGURE 5-1

The catalyst framework: design the catalyst for success

Identify the platform community	Establish a pricing structure	**Design the catalyst for success**	Focus on profitability	Compete strategically with other catalysts	Experiment and evolve
• Identify distinct groups that need each other	• Set separate prices for access and usage	• Attract multiple customer groups that need each other	• Study industry history	• Understand the dynamics of catalyst competition	• Know when to be first— and when to follow
• Determine why and how much they need each other	• Set prices to balance demand from two sides	• Promote interactions	• Use forecasts to enhance profitability	• Look for competition from different business models	• Control growth
• Evaluate who else is serving the community	• Price to grow slowly— at first	• Minimize transaction costs	• Anticipate competitor actions	• Leverage to attack	• Protect your back
• Compare a multisided business model with a single-sided one	• Pay customers to belong— sometimes	• Design for evolution	• Align interests internally and externally	• Consider cooperation	• Plan for what's next
	• Price for long-term profits				• Look out for the cops
Find out who needs whom— and why	**Shape participation and maximize profits**	**Draw customers and facilitate interactions**	**Visualize path toward long-term profit**	**Challenge existing catalysts and react to new catalyst threats**	**Pursue evolutionary strategy for growth**

sign is one aspect of that. Mori created walkways with outdoor art—even the benches are art of a sort—that encouraged people to meander around Roppongi Hills and visit its shops and restaurants. He avoided big open spaces between buildings that often go unused, as he learned from his experience with a smaller development in nearby Akasaka. Instead, he tried to create the "complexity and surprises" of neighborhoods such as Greenwich Village.[1]

3. **Minimize transaction costs.** People who come to live, work, and play at Roppongi Hills save a lot of time. They have confidence that Roppongi will have a certain kind of shop and restaurant. Most are concentrated on the first six

floors of Mori Tower. The shops and restaurants, too, are assured that most of the people walking by their establishments will be the kind of people who will appreciate them. That's because Mori established Roppongi Hills as the place to go in Tokyo for high-end eating and shopping.

4. **Design for evolution.** Unlike many of the catalysts we've seen, Roppongi Hills can't get much bigger. But its cachet could rise or fall and with it the value of living, working, or shopping there. Mori maintains tight control over this neighborhood to ensure that its luster remains and is perhaps even buffed over time. All spaces are leased rather than sold so that Mori can control the look and feel of the community. And since Mori earns his return by commanding high rents for the apartments, offices, and shop space, he has a strong interest in making sure that Roppongi Hills remains Tokyo's preeminent address.

While many have tried to create communities through large-scale urban renewal and failed, Minoru Mori managed to get the ingredients just right for a powerful catalytic reaction. He did it mainly through ingenious design. All catalysts need to follow the lessons that have made his city-within-a-city business model a success.

Task 1: Attract Multiple Groups

Catalyst communities all "live" on physical or virtual platforms.

Many physical platforms are, like Roppongi Hills, actual addresses where members of different customer groups go to meet and interact. Examples include the GUM shopping arcade in Moscow, the floor of the Chicago Mercantile Exchange, the Rialto Bridge in Venice, and the Viper Room on the Sunset Strip in Los Angeles. Other physical platforms are products that provide impersonal meeting places. Germany's *Stern*, Rupert Murdoch's Sky TV, and the *Hindustan Times* are examples of advertising-supported media that help advertisers and readers meet.

Virtual platforms are based on software code. Symbian OS, the computer operating system that is used on 71 percent of the smart phones shipped in the second quarter of 2006, is, in the end, electronic representations of 0s and 1s embedded in a chip.[2] This code helps provide a shared resource for a community of mobile phone users and developers of applications such as ringtones. Other virtual platforms such as Alibaba, the Chinese e-commerce portal, are similar but reside on the Web. With interconnected users, many of these portals offer communities that are almost as personal as Roppongi Hills.

Whether their meeting places are physical or virtual, personal or impersonal, catalysts find that expressly designing an appealing place for members of the community to get together is critical for starting and sustaining a successful reaction.

Sometimes, however, it is enough for a catalyst simply to create a single place—a focal point—where different customer groups can get together and interact. When two or more groups want to interact with each other, having a common place where group members know they can go for this purpose is sometimes enough to create a catalytic reaction. Most village markets are nothing more than a parking lot or town square where buyers and sellers come and trade. Lloyds of London began in late seventeenth-century London at a coffee shop that attracted seafarers and those interested in insuring their voyages. Craigslist—a centralized network of portals for urban areas with everything from classified ads to what's going on around town—also had a simple beginning. It started as Craig Neumark's list of interesting things to do in San Francisco that he e-mailed to his friends.

Catalysts should take several factors into consideration in selecting a focal point for getting their community together. They should make it as easy as possible for members of each customer group to get there. Village markets of old were centrally located for buyers and sellers, and modern shopping malls are located with commuting times firmly in mind. Roppongi Hills was built near the center of Tokyo with a major subway stop in it and two others within a four-minute walk. Catalysts should also make it especially easy for the customer group that is most desired by the other customer groups.

That's what Mori did by making sure that the wealthy workers and their highly profitable employers would want to locate in his minicity. They in turn attracted visitors and luxury shops and fine restaurants.

Of course, better design can often attract a greater number of customers looking for a match (see the box "The Power of a Network: Bungalow 8"). The Romans figured that out with the Forum. A multipurpose facility in the heart of Rome, the Forum was physically attractive and well organized for trading. As trading expanded, traders realized that more specialized markets would reduce congestion. Over time, markets were set up around the city for trading in wine, pork, vegetables, and other commodities. The London Stock Exchange (LSE) evolved from a gathering of traders at a coffee shop to a sophisticated, well-designed trading platform—one that has attracted broker-dealers, market makers, speculators, research providers, and other mutually dependent businesses that make financial exchanges work. The LSE has increased its attractiveness by providing platforms for trading in bonds and a range of other products in addition to shares of common stock. Craigslist, by contrast, moved beyond an e-mail list but remains simplicity personified. While other portals have gone glitzy, it remains a well-organized electronic bulletin board. Still, it at-

The Power of a Network: Bungalow 8

Amy Sacco has mastered the art of catalyst product design. After working as a hostess at several Manhattan nightspots, she opened her first club, Lot 61, in 1998. Bruce Willis, a friend, was the first celebrity to visit. After that, the celebrities came in droves. In its opening week, Lot 61 was named Best Bar in New York by *Time Out New York*. In 2001, Sacco opened Bungalow 8, which is so exclusive that even the stars of *Sex and the City* have had trouble passing muster.

Since Bungalow 8 has a capacity of only 125 people, Sacco has to ensure that only the "right" people enter. This she does mostly through her proxy, an enormous doorman who only allows the

tracted 13 million unique visitors a month in June 2006.[3] The genius of its design is in its convenience to both sides of the market.

Bundling is a critical design strategy for assembling audiences. It requires the deliberate mixing of different and diverse services on a single platform. Mori used it to ignite Roppongi Hills in April 2003. He devoted the top six floors of the Mori Tower to an art museum, a library, and other public spaces. The bottom six floors have a variety of shops (summarized in table 5-1) that, while all high-end, appeal to different sorts of people. There's a Virgin Entertainment complex that shows movies until 5 a.m. Many people who live in, work in, or just visit Roppongi Hills don't care about contemporary art or watching movies until dawn. But some people do, and others like the library, being able to shop at the chic women's clothing store Escada, or eating at L'Atelier, a famous French restaurant in the heart of Japan. By including many different uses of space in the design for this city within a city, Mori attracted a large and diverse audience. Others might have been attracted to Roppongi Hills precisely because it offered such diverse activities and distractions. What was important was that a sizable audience would be drawn to the development, which was then available to other shops. The result was that a highly diverse set of attractions made working and living—

very rich, the very famous, the very beautiful, and the very powerful to enter. Once in, this community of "it" people happily pay $1,200 for caviar and $50 for a cocktail just to rub shoulders with others just as rich, powerful, famous, and beautiful. Sacco not only has designed an attractive meeting place—Bungalow 8 is supposed to feel like the old Beverly Hills Hotel—but has used her network to ignite the catalytic reaction that has given the club its hip reputation and an enormously long life in an environment where clubs often come and go in a matter of weeks. "It's all about building up your network," Sacco explains. "Every time I meet someone who I think is cool or cute, I get their card."[4] Her Rolodex is probably one of the most coveted in town. And now so is her club.

TABLE 5-1

The shops and attractions of Roppongi Hills

Residence	Roppongi Hills residences
Movies	Virgin Toho Cinemas
Restaurants	Japanese, French, Chinese, Italian, ethnic, Western cuisine/grills, multinational cuisine, bakeries and cafés, bars, take-out delicatessen
Shops	Fashion wear, fashion accessories, household items, various shops: e.g., Hugo Boss, Versace, Folli Follie, Bouquet o! Bouquet
Services	Medical center/pharmacy, hair/beauty/massage salons, others
Wagon shops	Accessory à la Mode, Charms Fountain, La Rouge, Ray-Ban, Ty Store, et al.
Hotel	Grand Hyatt Tokyo
Art museum	Mori Art Museum
Office	Goodwill Group, Yahoo! Japan, Livedoor Company, Lehman Brothers Japan, Inc., Goldman Sachs
Corporate headquarters	TV Asahi
City plaza	Roppongi Hills Arena
Members-only club	Roppongi Hills Club (with eight restaurants and five bars)

and paying rent to Mori—highly desirable. "There's something for everyone" (who matters) is a smart strategy for catalysts because it builds up a valuable audience.

The *New York Times* provides another example of an effective bundling strategy. Every day the Gray Lady, as the paper is sometimes known, provides coverage of national and international news, sports, business, and arts and leisure. More specialized topics are covered on particular days: science on Tuesdays and dining on Fridays, for instance. Americans love their Sunday-morning papers, and many are devoted to the Sunday *New York Times*. That day's paper covers style and automobiles, as well as including book review and magazine supplements. Hardly anyone reads everything the newspaper offers. Studies of newspaper readership, in fact, find that newspaper sections are typically read by fewer than 60 percent of all readers. But by including all these features, the *New York Times* attracts 1.1 million readers, each of whom likes something in the paper. Bundling everything from retirement advice to crossword puzzles to wedding announcements helps the *Times* build an audience it sells to advertisers. (Of course, advertisers then pick the part of the paper that is most likely to attract the readers they care most about. The sports section doesn't have perfume and jewelry ads.)

Bundling different products or services on the same physical or virtual platform also saves money (see the box "The Economics of Bundling"). It often costs a considerable amount of money to maintain a platform and make it available to customers. The catalyst can often spread the fixed costs of the platform by expanding its use through bundling. The *New York Times* saves money and builds circulation by distributing the Sunday sports and style sections together rather than separately.

There are several lessons for designing a catalyst to attract multiple groups:

THE LESSONS

Identify a focal point that attracts members to a single location. For physical platforms, this is often a place that is convenient for members of multiple groups to get to.

Make it desirable to be at that location, not just to meet other customers. By offering many sources of value, the catalyst can attract more customers from each side; those customers then provide value to the other side.

Aggregate customers on each side by bundling features that appeal to different tastes within the target groups. It doesn't matter why those customers come to the platform; once they are there, they are a source of value of the other side—and thus to the platform.

The Economics of Bundling

Bundling is related to the architecture of product offerings. In important respects, product architecture is essentially assembling building blocks—like Legos—into a product with a given set of features or into several versions of products with varying features. Even as basic as the Model T appeared, it consisted of many Lego-like components—including Japan Black paint—that were assembled to make the final product: the first mass-produced car of the early twentieth century. As the industry evolved, automobile companies expanded their automobile bundles to include things that range from the seemingly mundane, such as air conditioning, to the seemingly exotic, such as a global positioning system (GPS) and satellite radio.

To take another example, the building blocks for cable television include mainly the channels offered. Cable television networks architect their products by creating alternative packages—basic and premium cable, for example—by bundling these channels. These product versions are also fluid in the sense that cable television companies routinely add and subtract channels from the "products" they offer, allowing different bundles to be assembled and different versions offered.

The basic strategic and design decisions faced by all businesses concern how to take the building blocks of features available to them and combine—or bundle—these blocks into the one or more versions of products that maximize profits, in essence answering two questions:

- *What features should be bundled together in a product?*
  The term feature means an aspect of a product that a consumer values. Should an automobile manufacturer, for example, make satellite radio standard on its cars? Should a software platform maker include antivirus software? Should a cable television company bundle a digital video recorder and video-on-demand service? The answer determines the optimal *product design.*

- *What versions of a product should be made available?*
  The term version refers to products that have different
  features although they may share a common base. Should
  an automobile maker offer one version of midsize sedans
  with satellite radio and another without? Should a search
  engine portal make a version available with premium paid
  content? Should a cable television company offer Voice
  over Internet Protocol (VoIP) and cable service? These
  versions determine the optimal *product line* or *product
  offering*.

Businesses, of course, address what bundles and versions to
make available to their customers all the time. Sometimes they
decide to give consumers many versions, as we all know from
shopping for jeans or wandering down the breakfast cereal aisle
at the local supermarket. Other times they give consumers few
versions. Consumers cannot subscribe to particular sections of
newspapers—all of them are bundled together into a single product. Apple tries to make sure you can't use your iPod with a
music service other than its iTunes store.

Most businesses, in practice, settle somewhere between these
two extremes. They offer consumers several alternative designs,
bundling multiple features together in each, but far fewer designs
than they could produce. In fact, the Model T was available in
several colors during its early years of production (1909–1914)
and again in its final two years of production (1926–1927). Most
car companies today offer many versions of their cars—with different options—although, in most cases, far fewer than they did
twenty years ago. Cable television companies, unlike newspapers, do not offer consumers an all-or-nothing deal. On the other
hand if you want ESPN—the popular American sports channel—
you may have to take a premium package that includes a bundle
of channels you will probably never watch.[5]

Task 2: Promote Interactions

Getting customers to visit the platform is at most half the battle. A catalytic reaction only occurs when members of the different groups interact with each other once they have arrived at the platform. Successful catalysts have discovered many ways for promoting these interactions. Some are less obvious than others.

Consider the strategy that glossy magazines such as *Vogue* follow for getting readers to interact with advertisers. To find the first page of the table of contents in the March 2006 issue, you would have to flip through twenty-two pages of advertisements. At the bottom of that first page, you would see that the table of contents is continued on page 30. You couldn't just turn to that page, though, because the subsequent pages aren't consistently numbered. So you would have to flip through another eight pages of advertisements. If you wanted to read the article in which Jeffrey Steingarten wonders whether a two-to-one ratio of butter to bread is an insult to the austere spirit of Zen, you would find it on page 246. That page, though, is hard to find without passing over many other advertisements. After reading two pages, you would find that the article is continued on page 390. Once again you would have to flip past many advertisements to find that page. (More than two-thirds of the pages have at least one advertisement.)

Vogue therefore makes it rather inconvenient for its readers. Of course, it does so because it expects that people will look at some of the intervening advertisements. By encouraging its readers to look at the ads for everything from Roberto Coin jewelry to Bose's SoundDock digital music system for iPods, it provides a more appealing product for these vendors. *Vogue* designs this platform for fashion-conscious women and the firms that want to sell to them to encourage interactions between the two sides.

THE LESSON

Catalysts should consider platform designs that make it easy or unavoidable for customers to interact with each other. The catalyst community can benefit from this overall even if some customers find being smashed together intrusive.

There are limits to how far catalysts can go in promoting interactions. In fact, we doubt that *Vogue* could be this aggressive unless its readers in fact enjoyed looking at pricey clothes and high-end accessories. Other magazines cater more to those who read, and their designs show this. In *People* magazine, for example, the pages are clearly numbered, it is easy to find the start of an article, and the story runs over consecutive pages, so you don't have to thumb through the magazine to get all the juicy details. Much of the advertising is grouped together at the front and the back, so readers who want to browse through it know where to go. Not surprisingly, *People* gets a much higher proportion of its revenues from readers—many of whom pay more than $100 a year for a subscription—than does *Vogue*.

THE LESSON

Catalysts must balance the short-run benefits of getting more interactions against the long-run costs of discouraging customers from coming to the platform. They should recognize that design decisions that encourage interactions might also discourage some customers from joining the platform.

Shopping mall design exemplifies the care that catalysts take in promoting interactions with a soft touch. Malls are usually designed to encourage shoppers to walk around and pass by as many storefronts as possible. Some, like Connecticut's Stamford Town Center, have the up and down escalators at opposite ends of a two-level space, so that people have to walk past stores when they change floors.

Alfred Taubman described the design philosophy that helped him create his mall empire: "You have two levels, all right? You have an escalator here and an escalator here. The customer comes into the mall, walks down the hall, gets on the escalator up to the second level. Goes back along the second floor, down the escalator, and now she's back where she started from. She's seen every store in the center, right? Now you put on a third level. Is there any reason to go up there? No."[6]

Many mall developers follow a marquee strategy to encourage foot traffic. Mall of America places its four anchor stores—Nordstrom, Sears, Macy's, and Bloomingdale's at the corners, as shown in figure 5-2.

FIGURE 5-2

First Mall of America floor plan

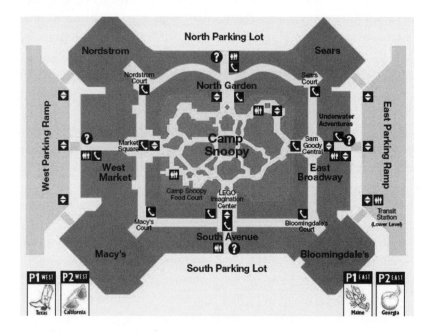

Source: "Mall of America: Store Directory and Map," Mall of America information website, http://www
.moainformation.com/pdfs/StoreDirectoryAndMap.pdf (used with permission by Mall of America).

It has an amusement park and other entertainment in the space in
between. It also has many carts for specialized merchandise that encourage people to wander around. Merchants value space at the mall
because they get a lot of traffic, while shoppers value both the selection of merchandise and the experience of walking through the mall.
Mall of America and similar malls could adopt designs that force
people to walk even more. For example, rather than having separate
exterior entrances to the anchor stores, it could force people to come
into a separate entrance and then walk past other shops to get to the
largest merchants. Instead, they have made it possible for people who
just want to go to Nordstrom to park near it and enter it directly.

EBay has taken many cues from bricks-and-mortar retailers in
designing its virtual shopping mall. It could have opted for an opening Web page that allows buyers to enter in the item they are search-

ing for. But such simplicity would have eliminated a critical aspect of the bricks-and-mortar shopping experience: serendipity. Experienced window-shoppers know that an important part of the experience is walking around and discovering interesting things to buy. Department stores and shopping malls "mix things up" to make these chance meetings of consumer preferences and merchandise more likely. EBay's Web site does the same. During the Christmas season of 2005, its front page presented shoppers with three options. On the left-hand side was the nod to simplicity: a list of shopping categories such as "dolls and bears" and "cars, parts & vehicles." In the middle there was a rotating list of items that focused on babies; there was also a locator that could find toys that would be appropriate for a child's age. Then on the right-hand side there was a list of suggestions ranging from remote control cars to engagement rings. Many catalysts pursue the same "complexity of surprises" that Mori did for Roppongi Hills.

THE LESSON

Serendipity is an important element of how consumers search for things to satisfy their needs. Physical and virtual spaces should encourage a degree of chance interactions between the different sides.

Of course, for many catalysts, interactions are best promoted directly. Exchanges and matchmakers, for example, are in the business of getting customers together quickly and efficiently. In chapter 2, we described the decidedly unsubtle approach of 8minuteDating, a speed-dating event that the organizers have designed to bring together men and women quickly and briefly. Other dating venues rely on the old-fashioned methods of dancing and drinking. Exchanges also provide very direct methods for encouraging interactions. The auctioneer has for millennia specialized in getting buyers and sellers to trade with each other and in achieving the best price for the seller.

THE LESSON

Catalysts in these areas should consider direct methods—including devising specific institutions such as the auctioneer—to promote interactions.

Task 3: Minimize Transaction Costs

As we saw in chapter 2, catalysts realize profits from identifying situations in which two types of customers would benefit from interacting with each other but can't do so efficiently on their own because of various transaction costs. Successful two-sided businesses design platforms that reduce these transaction costs and thereby make it possible for their customers to interact.

As we also discussed in chapter 2, catalysts are designed to make transactions easier and cheaper in four basic ways: they make information about customer groups available, provide search services for finding good matches between groups, bring the right combination of those groups together, and design and administer rules that reduce friction and make for productive catalytic reactions.

In the United States, for example, multiple listing services make it easy for buyers and sellers of homes to find each other. Most people who want to sell a home retain a real estate broker. The broker enters information on the house in a standard form. That "listing" is then put in a central repository, where it becomes available to other real estate brokers in the area.

Before the Internet became widely used, these listings were made available to buyers mainly through listing books, organized by price range, that were available in real estate brokers' offices. Buyers could go through the book to find properties they were interested in visiting. Today, most listings are available through Realtor.com. But information remains at the heart of bringing together buyers and sellers in a very easy and low-cost way.

Many sellers complain about the commissions they pay real estate brokers. No doubt the fact that brokers charge about 6 percent of the sale price regardless of market conditions or the effort required to sell a house is a source of puzzlement and concern for antitrust enforcers. Yet, in the end, most sellers find that it is worth paying the commission to have their properties made available to many potential buyers. Americans take this system for granted, but it is not universal. In France, for example, real estate brokers often have exclusive rights to list a property. If you want to have access to all the listings in an area, you have to use many brokers. While this may have other benefits, it drastically reduces the amount of information available to buyers. The result is that the French real estate market is less liquid than the U.S. market, and it takes much longer to sell a house there, on average.

Catalysts also reduce transaction costs by designing methods for selecting and aggregating certain types of customers on one side who are most valuable to customers on the other side.

The Japanese magazine *Leon* is designed to get the right set of men and merchants together. The right men are those between the ages of thirty-five and fifty-five who make more than 15 million yen ($140,000) annually. More audaciously, on its cover *Leon* says it "supports attractive, middle-aged men" (*moteru oyaji*). Its editor brags that it has no intellectual content and offers no lifestyle advice. Instead, it focuses on the interest (or perhaps daydreams) of its readership in attracting younger women and in the fashionable clothing and accessories that, supposedly, provide attractive bait.

While most of our readers may not be interested in the typical *Leon* browser, many advertisers are: they spend about 300 million yen ($2.55 million) each month for space in this 3-pound glossy. That is about $35.50 for each of the seventy thousand copies in circulation.[7] There is some evidence that the money is well spent. A *Japan Times* article reports, "In April [2004], they did a feature on small presents that men can give their dates. One was something called a Bijou Ring, made by the Swiss watchmaker Swatch. Throughout Japan, the rings sold out in two weeks."[8]

EBay takes a more mundane approach to getting the right buyers for its sellers. It tracks what people have purchased in the past. Also it allows buyers to register their interest in particular sorts of items. When sellers offer those items, eBay sends an e-mail to people in its community who it believes may desire them. EBay's $42.7 billion market capitalization (as of October 2006) is due in large part to having designed a platform for getting the right buyers and sellers together. Individuals and small businesses that sell obscure items—antique charge cards, for example—had little ability to find each other before eBay. Now it is easy.

In some cases, catalysts design search tools for members as a way of reducing transaction costs. As we've seen, the Manheim Auto Auction helps buyers and sellers search for a match by designing an auction process. Potential buyers first receive information as a result of having the opportunity to inspect the cars. Then Manheim has an auction in which interested buyers can bid on cars. The auction is a search mechanism that enables sellers to find the buyer who is willing to pay the most.

In other cases, catalysts do the search themselves and report the results to the customers. Customers on each side present information on their ideal match. The catalyst then searches through its data banks and finds appropriate matches. This is nothing new: village matchmakers have done this the low-tech way for millennia. Modern technology makes search far easier. Google uses its massive array of computers to target advertisements to people who are most likely to be interested in those pitches according to their search history. Most modern securities exchanges, such as Euronext in Paris or the International Securities Exchange in New York, receive orders electronically and use computers to connect buyers and sellers to each other or to market makers almost instantaneously. (Trading rules typically reflect the fact that, as one market participant put it, "to a computer, three seconds is an eternity.") Because all orders and transactions are handled by computers, it is possible for these exchanges to rapidly execute complex orders involving multiple securities and more than two parties. Similarly, computerization makes enforcement of a variety of rules and regulations easier by providing a precise record of who did what when.

Finally, well-designed catalysts establish rules and regulations that reduce friction among members of their community. Portobello Road in London is famous for its open-air market and the many shops that attract locals and tourists. The Portobello Antique Dealers Association has a special market that is open every Saturday morning at the junction of Portobello Road and Westbourne Grove. The association has adopted a code of ethics that requires members to post the price and provide as much information as possible about each item offered. It also prohibits members from misrepresenting antiques or otherwise confusing or misleading their customers. Customers can avoid the cost of taking dealers to court when they've gotten a bad deal or the frustration of knowing they have no realistic recourse: the association provides a dispute resolution service.

In order to provide low fares to consumers, Orbitz works hard to persuade airlines to provide it with their lowest fares available. At the same time, Orbitz also enforces a set of rules, mainly on its users, to encourage the airlines' participation in the platform. A purchase is finalized once issued. A user might have to pay a fee averaging $130 if she later wants to change or cancel an airline ticket, and she might be required to pay the price difference should the new fare be higher. In addition, tickets are nontransferable: a user can't change the name on a ticket or give the ticket to someone else to use.[9] And a user can't exchange a ticket from one airline to another airline. Most tickets purchased through Orbitz are nonrefundable, and some airlines don't allow changes at all.

Table 5-2 summarizes the ways catalysts reduce transaction costs and some of the results.

THE LESSON

Design your service to minimize transaction costs by providing centralized information. Prescreen members of the community so that they have to spend less time screening each other, and offer search methods that help customers get together.

TABLE 5-2

How catalysts reduce transaction costs

The tactics	The results
Provide information	Makes it easier to identify the best match from the customers on the platform
Get the "right" customers together	Reduces transaction costs by excluding undesirable matches from the platform
Provide search services	Facilitates finding the best match among those who have come to the platform
Design rules and regulations	Prevents bad behavior and provides a consistent experience

Task 4: Design for Evolution

A former senior officer of American Express told us the following story about the risks of forecasting. American Express's card business was doing extremely well in the 1960s. It had overtaken Diners Club despite having entered this catalyst category eight years after the pioneer. It had almost a million cards in circulation. Back then, the charge slips had to be sorted by hand. American Express was worried that with further expansion its back room would be overwhelmed by the task. It hired a well-known management consulting firm to advise it on what to do. The consultants concluded that the card market had matured and American Express wouldn't grow much past a million cards. Not long afterward, American Express had 2 million cards in circulation. Once again it was advised by the same consultants that the market had matured and growth was over. And once again American Express soon found that it had issued another million cards.

While these management consultants could be criticized for their lack of foresight, their failure to predict the future evolution of the card business is not surprising. It is hard to forecast the evolution of catalytic reactions, particularly novel ones, dependent as they are on positive feedbacks among multiple customer groups. If these feedback effects come in with force, they can power rapid growth. If they are slow to start, or don't take hold at all, the catalytic reaction will peter out. What is a catalyst to do given this inherent unpredictability?

THE LESSON

Design a flexible platform that can be expanded or contracted easily.

While American Express and Diners Club did this well, MasterCard and Visa did it better. They designed cooperative networks that combined highly centralized hubs for authorizing and settling transactions with highly decentralized spokes for providing services to cardholders and merchants. Each cooperative established a card brand and operated the hub. The members—individual financial institutions—issued branded cards to consumers and signed up merchants to accept branded cards. (While some banks still handle both cardholders and merchants, over time most banks and other firms have specialized in one side or the other.) Starting with a few hundred banks in the mid-1960s, in 2005 MasterCard had twenty-five thousand participating banks and Visa had twenty-one thousand.[10] As demand expanded, the design of this platform made it easy to bring additional capacity into the industry, particularly outside the United States. As important, during periods of weak demand, the platform has contracted, or slowed its growth, with minimal disruption as some members discontinued their card programs and sold their portfolios to stronger members.

Linux—the open source operating system that has given Microsoft global heartburn—has also shown the importance of design. Linus Torvalds posted ten thousand lines of code for the "kernel" of this operating system in 1991. He made it available under an *open source license* that enables others to revise, embellish, and redistribute the code so long as they agree to make the entire program available to others just as Torvalds did for them. In practice, Torvalds and others have carefully managed the evolution of Linux by deciding which revisions to accept in the standard version. The design of Linux makes it relatively easy for contributors to add modules of code and for the operating system to grow over time. As of 2001, the most popular release of Linux, Red Hat, had 30 million lines of code. Since 1991, Linux has grown from a software platform for a few hobbyists to a platform with more than 29 million users worldwide and more than ten thousand applications.[11] Many developers are now developing applications for Linux that they sell to users. (We discuss Linux in more detail in chapter 7.)

Roppongi Hills can't easily expand like Linux or MasterCard. It is self-contained on its 11.6-hectare site. Yet new life is constantly breathed into this community through continual replacement of merchants and restaurants—about 10 percent changed over in the first three years. And the managers of Roppongi Hills can influence who leaves—leases can be terminated after two years by mutual consent—and who comes in—the type and quality of store is critical in the decision of who gets a lease. Mori designed Roppongi Hills to sustain a catalytic reaction between workers, residents, merchants, restaurants, and visitors. Although he can't make this city within a city bigger, over time he can make it better or at least prevent it from losing the positive feedbacks among the members of the community that have made it a success so far.

Some catalysts need to contract in size—in some dimension— and have the flexibility to do so. The *Atlantic Monthly*, which publishes a high-brow collection of fiction and nonfiction articles, was founded in Boston in 1857, making it one of the oldest continuously published magazines in the United States. Like many magazines of its kind, it has trouble making a profit and depends on benefactors. However, with mounting losses, the magazine decided it needed to earn more from subscribers. It increased subscription prices from $15 in 2003 to almost $50 in 2006. Circulation dropped by 25 percent, from five hundred thousand copies, shortly after prices were increased (circulation rose somewhat after that initial drop).[12] With fewer subscribers, its advertising revenue dropped, unsurprisingly, between those years: by about 21 percent, from $31.7 million to $25 million.[13] The net result, though, was a financially healthier magazine (though still one that relied on a benefactor).

Design and the Catalyst Framework

The importance of design in the catalyst framework can be seen in the often frustrating efforts of catalyst entrepreneurs to introduce a smart card—a plastic card with a computer chip—to replace the ubiquitous magnetic stripe cards that now dominate the payment card system in the United States.

People have been paying with plastic for more than thirty years now. The plastic payment card is a masterful piece of design. It weighs about 7 grams and fits easily into your wallet. The magnetic stripe on the back provides a simple interface with card readers, the signature line a cheap method for identifying the holder, and the embossed numbers on the front a convenient record of your account number. By agreeing on standards for the consumer's card and the merchant's readers, the card systems accelerated a catalytic reaction that now drives more than 200 million card transactions a day around the world.[14]

The signature line has been technologically obsolete since the 1980s, when the smart card—a plastic card with a computer chip—became available. Yet, in the United States, no one has developed a successful business model for the smart card that appeals to consumers and merchants. Several attempts have failed as merchants refused to upgrade their technology to take the newfangled cards, and consumers found little reason to carry a card they couldn't use.

Many entrepreneurs remain convinced, however, that they can come up with an even better design for paying for things digitally. PayByTouch, for example, is trying to replace plastic with flesh. People register one of their fingerprints and provide details on the checking account or credit card account to which they want the transaction billed. When they want to pay, they simply press their finger on a device at the merchant. PayByTouch authenticates their fingerprint and then takes care of settling the merchant and consumer accounts. Another company we are working with has developed software technology that can enable a variety of computer devices to replace plastic. One device it is considering is a bit larger than an Apple iPod nano and can authenticate fingerprints.

The challenge all these entrepreneurs face is coming up with a design that solves the chicken-and-egg or hen-and-rooster problem that we discussed earlier. Young people may like to be able to wave their iPods at a special terminal to pay for things, but merchants won't install those terminals unless a lot of customers want to pay this way.

One way to crack the catalyst code is to modify the design of an existing platform that serves the customer groups the catalyst is trying to attract. That's how MasterCard and Visa are trying to introduce contactless cards in the United States—plastic cards with a wireless chip that allows them to be read when they are waved past a special card reader. These systems are issuing cards that have both contactless chips and magnetic stripes so consumers can continue to use these cards at merchants with traditional readers. They are also trying to persuade industries that are just starting to take plastic, such as fast food, to install contactless readers. The new card design potentially reduces the transaction cost for both cardholder and merchant.

I-mode followed a similar leverage strategy in Japan. It had its phone suppliers add the FeliCa contactless chip (developed by Sony) to i-mode phones, and it added a payment feature to these phones. With this base of payment-enabled phones, it was able to persuade merchants to install contactless readers. To pay for things, a consumer can simply enter a PIN on her i-mode FeliCa phone and wave it at one of these readers; i-mode takes care of paying the merchant and billing the consumer. Since it introduced this technology in July 2004, more than 2.4 million FeliCa-equipped cell phones have been sold, and they are accepted at more than 26,000 retail outlets and 3,900 vending machines.[15]

I-mode's success, like Roppongi Hills', is evidence of the importance of product design to bring together the participants in two-sided and multiple-sided markets. A successful product design for catalysts has to get the multiple customer groups on board and interacting with each other. But if the design only appeals to one group, while the other sees it as too inconvenient or burdensome, the catalytic reaction can never take place.

The magnetic stripe on the back of your American Express card has survived for so long in the face of technological change

TABLE 5-3

Designing the catalyst for success

Tasks	Lessons
Attract multiple groups that need each other.	• Make it desirable to be at that location, not just to meet other customers. • Bundle features that appeal to different tastes.
Promote interactions.	• Make it easy for both sides of a market to connect. • Encourage a degree of chance interactions. • Use devices such as an auctioneer to promote interactions.
Minimize transaction costs.	• Centralize information to minimize search and transaction costs.
Create evolutionary design.	• Make it easy to expand or contract the platform.

because it worked well enough to get cardholders and merchants transacting with each other. The check with a signature for verification has lasted even longer—more than six centuries—because it too is a simple design that works well enough for banks, businesses, and consumers. But perhaps both have survived because no one has yet come up with a design that would persuade both sides of the market to abandon their old habits and technology.

If its pricing and product design can persuade the right groups to come together and interact, an aspiring catalyst has cleared a significant hurdle. At that point, having completed the tasks outlined in table 5-3, it still must demonstrate that it can generate a *profitable* catalytic reaction. We take up this element of the catalyst framework in the next chapter.

6

Focus on Profitability

Profit is not the proper end and aim of management—
it is what makes all of the proper ends and aims possible.

—DAVID PACKARD

CHRISTMAS 2005. THE MUST-HAVE/CAN'T-GET PRODUCT IS the new Xbox video game console. It lists for $299.99. Shoppers line up and inventories vanish. People turn to eBay, where some boxes reportedly have gone for as much as $10,000 (though fully loaded with games and more). The box is hot because it packs lots of cool features that the market-leading Sony PlayStation doesn't have yet—Sony is still almost a year away from releasing its new console. And there are new games that use the Xbox's latest tricks. One of the most popular is *Fight Night Round 3*, made by Electronic Arts.

This market reception was a nice present for the Microsoft Home and Entertainment Division. It had placed a huge financial bet on its Xbox creation four years earlier. Its goal: to get into the huge video game console business that Sony had all but sewn up. Its prospects: slim but better than none. The video game console business had a history of leapfrog competition in which one firm would lead the category for a number of years until another firm came up with something better. Yet Microsoft had tried and failed to get into the video game business before, and, after all, what did it know about making hardware? Its alternative: not attractive. Though dedicated initially to gaming, the Sony PlayStation was a fast, capacious computer with a highly able operating system aimed at the potentially huge market for computer-based home entertainment. If Microsoft wanted a chance at that market, it had to make one more try at the game business.

By the summer of 2006, it looked as if Microsoft might succeed. It had shipped 1.8 million of its new consoles between April and June 2006. With consumers having more than 5 million Xbox 360 consoles worldwide, it had established itself as the solid number two in the video game business, with a shot at number one.[1]

It was, however, still bleeding cash: the Microsoft Home and Entertainment Division lost more than $1.3 billion in the fiscal year ending June 30, 2006.[2] And it faced an impending counterattack from the industry leader—Sony, whose third-generation consoles were predicted to hit the shelves in November just in time for the Christmas 2006 season.

Whether Microsoft will see any returns on its multibillion-dollar Xbox investment—let alone enough to compensate for the huge risks it has borne—is likely to remain an open question through the first decade of the twenty-first century. The software giant has found, as have many other catalysts, that igniting a catalytic reaction doesn't guarantee a reasonable return on investment, let alone a reward for taking on substantial risk. Entrepreneurs must understand not only the dynamics of how a platform can attract communities of customers who need one another, but also how that platform can eventually secure profits.

Profit, of course, is essential to all businesses. But in a multisided business, profitability is a tricky achievement. It is, of course, essential to get and keep the different groups on board the platform and to encourage members of these groups to interact with each other using the platform's services, as we have discussed. But the timing with which each side gets on board, and the speed with which they attract each other, can make the difference between profit and loss. Competition—from established catalysts that provide similar services or from imitators of a new two-sided business—also threatens the quest for profits. Moreover, as we discussed in chapter 4, establishing the right pricing strategy for a successful catalyst often means that one side of the business is offered to customers at a very low fee or even for free, generating little, if any, revenue and dragging down profit. Inside the organization, the balance between the profit- and loss-making sides requires careful attention to how employees are motivated and compensated. Employees must have a stake in the profitability of the overall catalytic reaction, not just part of it. All these challenges make a steady focus on profitability critical for planning and managing a new catalyst business—and thus a crucial element of the catalyst framework (see figure 6-1).

This chapter uses the video game industry, with some supplementary insights drawn from the payment card industry, to highlight the lessons that all catalysts must learn to secure a long-term return from their investments in bringing communities together. Specifically, we examine four key tasks that can help prospective catalysts realize their potential for profits and, as importantly, know when to modify their pricing models or even close down a lively catalytic reaction when profits are beyond reach:

1. Study the history of the industry to learn why catalysts succeed or failed in this arena in the past.

2. Use history and experience to forecast the evolution of profits under alternative scenarios, especially concerning the degree and speed of positive feedbacks.

3. Anticipate multisided strategies from incumbent catalysts and new entrants, and plan your best countermoves.

4. Align interests both internally and externally so that all employees and all other members of the catalyst community feel they have a stake in the long-term profitability of the company.

FIGURE 6-1

The catalyst framework: focus on profitability

Identify the platform community	Establish a pricing structure	Design the catalyst for success	Focus on profitability	Compete strategically with other catalysts	Experiment and evolve
• Identify distinct groups that need each other	• Set separate prices for access and usage	• Attract multiple customer groups that need each other	• Study industry history	• Understand the dynamics of catalyst competition	• Know when to be first—and when to follow
• Determine why and how much they need each other	• Set prices to balance demand from two sides	• Promote interactions	• Use forecasts to enhance profitability	• Look for competition from different business models	• Control growth
• Evaluate who else is serving the community	• Price to grow slowly—at first	• Minimize transaction costs	• Anticipate competitor actions	• Leverage to attack	• Protect your back
• Compare a multisided business model with a single-sided one	• Pay customers to belong—sometimes	• Design for evolution	• Align interests internally and externally	• Consider cooperation	• Plan for what's next
	• Price for long-term profits				• Look out for the cops
Find out who needs whom—and why	**Shape participation and maximize profits**	**Draw customers and facilitate interactions**	**Visualize path toward long-term profit**	**Challenge existing catalysts and react to new catalyst threats**	**Pursue evolutionary strategy for growth**

Task 1: Study Industry History

History can tell the catalyst much about what's worked, what hasn't, what's failed, and why. One might think that successful catalysts have such original business models that no history is useful in their analysis. But such originality is very rare. Great catalysts, like great scientists, generally achieve breakthroughs in large part because they are standing on the shoulders of giants who have gone before them. And many of the most successful businesses were built by tweaking another's insight to set off a much more powerful and sustainable catalytic reaction than their predecessor's.

When it decided to enter the video game business, Microsoft could learn a lot from the previous quarter century's history. The industry hadn't started with a multisided strategy. In 1972, a now-defunct television manufacturer, Magnavox, launched Odyssey, the first game system. Odyssey came with twelve games and hooked up to a television set. Magnavox's strategy, though, was too clever by half: it misled consumers into thinking they needed a Magnavox television to use the system, thereby discouraging the many consumers who didn't want a Magnavox. It sold about one hundred thousand game systems through its stores and other retailers, but Odyssey soon fizzled.

Meanwhile, Atari had built up a successful business selling microprocessor-based arcade game systems to bars. Its *Pong* game demanded just enough dexterity to be enjoyed by tipsy patrons. Atari then created a home version of the game. Sears, alone among retailers, took a gamble on it despite the Odyssey fiasco. *Pong* flew off its shelves during the 1975 Christmas season, and the home video game industry was born.

The video game business was decidedly single sided back then. Companies like Atari made systems that bundled the computer hardware, operating systems, and games into a single box. They bought or developed all the components themselves and then sold their systems to home users. The two-sided model became feasible because of changes in technology and design.

An Atari competitor came out in 1976 with a system that put the games on separate cartridges so people could buy additional games to play with their consoles. Atari followed suit a year later and roared ahead as a result of making the popular arcade game *Space Invaders* available as one of its cartridges. Atari's success was also partly driven by its razor blade pricing strategy. It sold the consoles for a bit less than their manufacturing cost and made its profits from creating a stream of games that it could sell to console owners. It sold 15 million consoles between 1979 and 1982, when it was riding high with *Space Invaders* and other popular games. Atari still had a single-sided strategy: although cartridges were available separately, they were all developed and sold by Atari.

But what stopped others from entering the lucrative game cartridge business? Not much, as it turns out, and the market was soon flooded with games that weren't produced by the console makers. Atari and the other console makers didn't have any way to charge these competitors. The free-riding game makers cut into their sales and often made poor games that reflected badly on the consoles. The video game industry soon tanked, and Atari headed into a long period of decline that persisted even when the industry returned to health.

Nonetheless, Atari's video game consoles seemed to be the basis of a successful catalyst. After all, its video games created a legion of addicted players. And game writers, albeit of varying quality, were eager to create new products. But Atari had failed to devise a long-term plan to generate profits. The problem it faced was a variation on the chicken-and-egg problem we have seen several times. Consumers wouldn't pay much for consoles unless they knew there were good games for them. Game makers might be eager to write games for popular consoles, but the console makers had no guarantee that the games would please customers or any way to charge the game writers for using their platform.

In 1983 Nintendo cracked the catalyst code by creating a console that came with what amounted to built-in quality control. Its solution came in the form of a security chip in the console. A game would play on Nintendo's system only if its developer got the key for this chip and used a Nintendo-made cartridge to house the game. In a single stroke, Nintendo figured out how to motivate both sides of the video game market, protecting consumers from lousy games while encouraging the best game makers to write games for its proprietary platform.

But access to the Nintendo platform wasn't free for developers. Nintendo charged game makers a royalty of 20 percent of sales. Nintendo struck deals with a few high-quality developers that were eager to participate in a console that offered its consumers a "seal of quality" on games that could be played only on Nintendo.

For its 1983 launch, Nintendo still made many of the games itself, including the hit *Mario Brothers*. That was in part because it initially couldn't get more than four developers on board. Knowing that its game revenues weren't going to be creamed off by free-riding developers, it sold its console at a loss to get game users on board its platform, and it looked for profits from its game sales and royalties.

This strategy, together with a technologically advanced system that consumers liked, ignited a catalytic reaction that was both powerful and profitable. Game developers started flocking to Nintendo. The stock of Nintendo-compatible games increased, making the console more valuable to consumers. Nintendo had found the right path to profitability. And the video game industry made a critical transition from a one-sided to a two-sided, catalytic business model.

Nintendo stayed in the lead by and large until 1996, when Sony leapfrogged because of a better console technology. Sony employed the same two-sided strategy: charging game makers a proportion of sales while offering its game players a pipeline of high-quality and exclusive content. Figure 6-2 illustrates the competition between Nintendo and Sony over time.

The success of the Nintendo model was particularly striking because it turned the catalyst formula that had achieved such fabulous

FIGURE 6-2

Nintendo versus Sony, 1982–2005

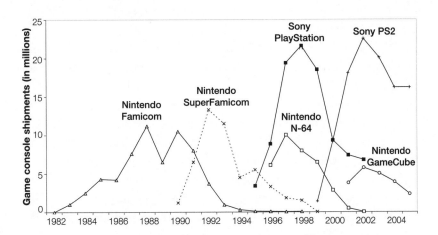

Sources: Yoshiko Motoyama, "Nintendo—At a Crossroads," Morgan Stanley Equity Research, September 6, 2004 (used with permission by Morgan Stanley); Sony company data; Nintendo company data.

success for Microsoft's operating system on its head. Remember, a video game console system is very similar to a personal computer system. They are both computers with operating systems on which applications run. In fact, many developers have written games for both personal computers and video game consoles.

Microsoft's strategy to ignite its PC operating system business was to encourage competition among the PC makers but to make software services available for free to developers. The fact that software developers wanted to write software programs that worked on the Microsoft operating system helped make that system so attractive to PC users. Microsoft didn't feel the need to charge developers a percentage of their sales for being able to use the operating system.

In 1991 Trip Hawkins, who today runs the giant game developer Electronic Arts, thought he saw a catalyst opportunity in using Microsoft's model. He founded 3DO on the idea that he would do for video games what Bill Gates had done for PCs. 3DO had a game technology that some thought was the best available at the time. Instead of making its own consoles, it licensed the technology to manufacturers in return for royalties—just as Microsoft licensed Windows. Several major manufacturers agreed to make 3DO's Multiplayer console. And with this stream of revenue coming in from hardware makers, Hawkins figured his company could undercut the royalties Nintendo charged to developers by 80 percent in order to spur them to write games for 3DO.

This seemed like a brilliant strategy. With a flood of new, high-end games in the stores, consumers would wait in line to get the sophisticated 3DO console needed to play them. Interesting theory, but it didn't work. The hardware makers, which had to pass the royalties on to customers and make profit on the boxes, sold the Multiplayer for around $700. Competing consoles were going for less than $200. Games for the Multiplayer didn't materialize either. The developers weren't willing to invest in writing games since they weren't convinced enough consumers would buy the pricey boxes. This is the sort of vicious cycle that strangles catalysts in the crib. As it did 3DO.

The failure of 3DO, however, proved to be an extremely valuable demonstration project for future game developers—especially

Microsoft. It showed that the catalyst formula for PC operating system software didn't work in the game world. Game players liked using a console that took measures to ensure the quality of its games, but they weren't willing to spend a fortune on it.

The brief history of video games was something Microsoft was in no position to ignore when, in 1999, it launched "Project Midway" to challenge Japanese dominance in this arena. Microsoft recognized that its two-sided rivals had helped create a vibrant industry of game developers, and its own history taught it the potential value of such complementors. But, as in Trip Hawkins' case, Microsoft's first instincts were that the road to riches in video games was the same one it had traveled in personal computers: make a great software platform; license it to hardware makers and get hardware prices down through competition; and let developers write games for free using the services provided by the platform. The Microsoft team had watched 3DO try this and fail miserably. But they initially thought that 3DO's mistake had been letting manufacturers price the console too high.

Still, history had made them cautious. Rather than plowing ahead with the PC model, they tested the assumptions behind their three-sided strategy. As the company approached hardware makers and game developers, they quickly discovered that the 3DO lessons had to be heeded. The hardware makers, a key part of the catalyst community, in fact rebuffed the software behemoth. The manufacturers knew that video game consoles were typically sold at a loss, and they had no way to recoup such losses through game sales. Michael Dell, whose company was the leader in making PCs, put it this way: "When Sony cuts the prices on their PlayStations, their stock price goes up. Every time I cut prices, my stock price goes down. If you don't understand why that happens, you don't understand the console business. I understand why this is strategic to Microsoft. I don't understand why this is strategic to Dell."[3]

So Microsoft had a hard time getting a supplier to make the consoles for it. Moreover, it found that game developers were no more interested in writing games for Microsoft's product than they were for 3DO's. Even if Microsoft didn't require them to pay royalties, they faced the prospect of making large investments in games only to find out that few households had bought the new console. The chicken-and-egg problem still had to be solved.

And so it didn't take long for Microsoft to accept the same basic route to profitability as its Japanese rivals. Build an integrated console that includes the hardware and the software, sell the console at a loss to attract many end users, let developers know that's the plan to convince them that writing games for those end users will be profitable, and seek profits from games developed in-house and from royalties from third-party games.

Still Microsoft, like Nintendo in games (and Palm in handheld devices), couldn't count on the developer community to help it launch the Xbox. As for all catalysts, getting the business off the ground would be a challenge. Few developers wanted to take the risk of writing games for an unproven console that at the time existed only on paper. The best way to develop the other side of the community was for Microsoft (like Palm and Nintendo) to make or acquire some of its own games. Microsoft promptly went out and acquired some successful third-party game developers. When the Xbox was introduced in 2001, it had fifteen games available for it; Microsoft had developed three of them itself, while the other twelve were created by independent developers such as Tecmo and Bizarre Creations.[4]

History was very useful to Microsoft. It is plausible that had it entered the market for video games before 3DO, it would have stuck with the PC model—and failed. Its careful observation of what was already working in the industry showed it that catalyst models, even in what seem to be very similar businesses, can operate very differently.

THE LESSON

Don't assume that what worked as a catalyst in a related industry will work as well for your business. Study the history of any sector you consider entering, and find out why some business models worked and others didn't.

By following this lesson, Microsoft had narrowed down the paths to profitability. It knew what wouldn't ignite a profitable catalytic reaction. The question remained—what would?

Task 2: Use Forecasts to Enhance Profitability

Like a mountain climber taking on a new peak, a would-be catalyst must know what to expect. No sensible climber would set off without having some idea of how high the peak was, what challenges he might face along the way, or some indication of when to give up. No sensible entrepreneur would set off a catalytic reaction without some idea of how long it would take to achieve profitability, what losses could be expected along the way, and when he should recognize that it's time to back away from failure. To have guideposts on whether they are heading to a profit peak or diving into a chasm, catalysts must have forecasts of the growth of each side of their businesses, how that growth will affect the growth of the other side of their businesses, and the nature and intensity of the interactions between the customer sides. History can inform such forecasts; experience must be used to revise them—sometimes drastically.

American Express didn't have much history to go on when it decided to get into the charge card industry in the mid-1950s. It could hardly emulate Diners Club, which had started small and learned the business. By the time American Express launched its card, Diners Club had 750,000 cardholders and 17,000 merchants taking its card. American Express had to rapidly scale up both sides of the business to mount a serious challenge to the incumbent. And so it did, by signing up 17,500 establishments by its launch in October 1958 and buying several hundred thousand cardholders from existing programs, such as that operated by the American Hotel Association.[5] This, together with the American Express reputation, ignited a catalytic reaction.

And then the big losses started rolling in. American Express hadn't learned the business of granting credit or dealing with merchants. By 1961 its card had lost millions, with no end in sight. American Express had to decide whether it could find a path to profitability. It concluded it couldn't and tried to sell the business to Diners Club. The two card giants reached a deal, but it fell apart in the wake of concerns—which seem laughable in hindsight—that antitrust authorities would oppose the consolidation of the two largest players. Instead, American Express found a new manager for the division, George Waters, who steered the catalytic reaction to profitability. After some analysis, Waters concluded that consumers valued the Amex card and would be willing to pay higher annual fees than Amex and its competitors were charging without dropping their cards. So Amex raised cardholder fees by more than 30 percent, from $6 to $8 and then to $10. At the same time, Amex imposed tough discipline on people who didn't pay their bills on time. It experienced little resistance from cardholders, and as a result, this side of the business became less of a drag on earnings. The card program turned profitable within a year and has been a major driver of Amex's profits ever since.

This serendipitous decision to remain in the card business illustrates an important lesson for catalysts. Small changes in pricing and other strategies can have enormous consequences for profitability. If a multisided business isn't on the path to profitability despite having ignited a catalytic reaction, it should, before turning back, consider modifying its business model in light of experience. In doing so, it must be careful not to stall its growth. In practice, that often means determining whether it is possible to raise prices to one or both groups of customers without experiencing significant defections that could end the catalytic reaction.

By the time Sears started the Discover Card system in 1986— the first new system in two decades—the economics of the payment card industry were better understood. Card catalysts had to endure massive losses initially while signing up cardholders and merchants. And it was understood that to make money on credit cards that allowed people to finance their balances over time, the issuer needed people who paid their bills on time (those who didn't were default risks) but not in full (so the issuer could earn profits from finance charges) and who charged a lot (so the issuer could earn more merchant fees and finance charges). Finding these ideal people was like drilling for oil. It took time and money to develop a portfolio of profitable cardholders.

Sears had the benefit of this knowledge when it drew up the business plan for its new card venture. So it wasn't surprised when it lost hundreds of millions of dollars in the first few years. It was confident that by getting merchants and cardholders on board its new system and finding profitable cardholders, its enormous investment would pay off. According to industry analysts and several news accounts, Discover was one of the greatest business success stories of the 1980s. It had almost 38 million cardholders by 1990, making it the largest credit card issuer by number of cards, the second largest (behind Citicorp) by outstanding loans to consumers, and the third largest (behind American Express and Citicorp) by dollars charged on the cards. Its cards were accepted at more merchants than American Express's. While it remains in fourth place among card systems in the United States, with less than one-third of the annual charges of American Express, Discover was a highly profitable investment for Sears, which sold off the business as part of Dean Witter in 1993. (It is part of Morgan Stanley as of 2006.)

Not all start-up catalysts have the wealth of information Discover had. But, when possible, multisided businesses should carefully model their profit trajectories, understand the duration and depth of losses before realizing a return on their investment, and assess the sensitivity of the calculations to the growth in demand on both sides of the business and the nature and intensity of attraction between the two sides.

Microsoft was like Sears in having a long history of successful and unsuccessful ventures to study before taking the plunge into an established catalyst industry. Microsoft seemed to clear the first hurdle by getting Xboxes into the hands of households. The company delivered its first Xbox to the stores on November 15, 2001. It listed for $299, matching the Sony PlayStation. And sure enough, there were hit games for it—like *Halo: Combat Evolved.* And in the first two months, Microsoft met its goal of selling 1.5 million boxes in the U.S. market.[6]

But staying on the profitability path required continual fine-tuning. Because the catalyst reaction required constantly keeping the bond between game players and game makers strong, Microsoft paid very close attention to price and consumer response. During those first few critical weeks, Microsoft cut the prices on Xboxes several times to entice consumers. It knew from studying the industry that a failure to get enough devices into homes would doom the entire enterprise. At this stage, making sure that it could ignite and sustain a catalytic reaction was far more critical than earning short-term profits.

During those first two months, U.S. Xbox purchasers bought an average of three games, although these were mainly games developed or acquired by Microsoft. Not enough third parties had yet signed on, and those that had weren't making much use of the Xbox's distinctive features. The situation was even worse in Japan, with its large game-playing audience. Few developers signed on, and the Xbox did poorly on Sony's and Nintendo's home turf.

Having studied the industry, Microsoft understood and expected this bumpy start. Importantly, it wasn't expecting an immediate burst of profit. Instead, the company predicted that it wouldn't turn a profit for three years, and that turned out to be a good estimate. Microsoft's game division had its first profitable quarter at the end of 2004. However, losses reappeared in 2005 as a result of the launch of the new Xbox and have continued through the end of fiscal 2006, resulting in cumulative operating losses of $3.9 billion.[7] Figure 6-3 shows Xbox revenue and losses over time.

Anyone who has worked with start-ups and their backers knows that the more innovative the business, the harder it generally is to forecast adoption and success. And as we will see in chapter 8, the nature of catalytic reactions makes their growth and profit potential particularly difficult to predict. But all catalysts, and especially those that can rely on the rich experience of other multisided businesses in the same industry, should take the following lessons to heart.

THE LESSONS

Make realistic forecasts of the level and duration of losses. These not only will help assess whether the investment is worth it but will provide a guidepost in deciding whether to persist in the face of red ink.

Evaluate the risks. Starting a catalyst often requires a considerable investment. Make sure that the likelihood of sustaining a catalytic reaction in the face of possible competition can deliver a sound risk-adjusted return on your capital. The key risks are whether it is possible to even ignite a catalytic reaction and whether a successful one can generate profits.

FIGURE 6-3

Revenue and operating income of Microsoft Home and Entertainment Division, 2002–2006

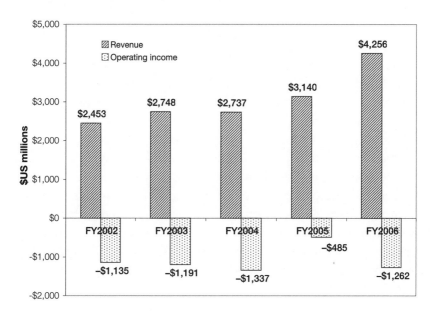

Source: Microsoft SEC filings

Keep your eye on the goal of having a long-term, sustainable, and profitable catalytic reaction. Adjust prices and design even if they deepen short-term losses, so long as they contribute to reaching this long-term objective.

Know when to cut and run. Significant shortfalls in getting customers on board from each side suggest that you have chosen the wrong multisided strategy for your catalyst business.

Task 3: Anticipate Competitor Actions

Every once in a while, someone comes up with an idea that is so innovative that there really are no competitors they have to worry about—at least for a while. When Frank McNamara introduced the payment card, he was competing mainly with cash and checks—neither of which had a sponsor with the interest or the ability to mount a response to his gnat of a payment device. Maybe Diners Club would ignite a profitable catalytic reaction, maybe it wouldn't; but either way, the company didn't need to worry much about the reaction of existing competitors. Imitators were the major threat to Diners Club if it succeeded. In assessing future profitability, it needed to consider how quickly these would appear, their likely strengths, and how it could respond.[8]

Many aspiring catalysts are, of course, imitators that find themselves challenging an already successful multisided firm. Just as the new catalyst needs to anticipate imitative entry, the challengers to the pioneering catalyst need to forecast how the incumbent will react. When American Express decided to go ahead with a card program, it had to anticipate how Diners Club would respond and how it could use its strengths—in particular, its worldwide base of travel offices and merchant relationships—to gain a competitive edge.

Firms that start new multisided businesses face the same issues as firms that start new single-sided ones in anticipating and responding to competitors. Rivals to the new business may lower their prices, try to lock up assets that the new business needs to compete, or simply copy the innovations made by the entrant. However, new catalysts face issues that traditional firms don't encounter. We focus on those critical issues here. Chapter 7 presents a broader discussion of competitive issues that catalysts face. Here we examine offensive strategies for an established catalyst trying to fend off new competition and defensive strategies for a new rival trying to survive in an established multisided industry. Both involve the same basic issues—just from different perspectives. Understanding these strategies is essential for making sure that there is an achievable path to profitability and for staying on this path.

Many catalyst businesses have a side that is most critical for their success, and that side is generally the focus of competitive battles. If customers on one side have to invest more to make use of the platform, they will tend to insist that the platform have the other side lined up already. That's the case with video games. Game publishers have to invest considerable resources developing games for a new console. They won't do that, as we've discussed, unless the console maker convinces them that enough consumers will have its new box.

Consequently, getting consoles into the hands of consumers is essential for survival in the video game industry. Microsoft had to commit to low console prices to get independent game developers to write games for the first version of its Xbox. Not surprisingly, when Microsoft's Xbox was introduced, Sony dropped the price on its PlayStation console from $299 to $199 in the United States and from 38,000 yen to less than 30,000 yen in its home market of Japan. Microsoft anticipated this response and quickly dropped its prices to match.[9]

THE LESSON

Catalysts should be prepared for stiff price competition for the most critical customer group from established multisided businesses and new entrants.

Key customer groups don't always coincide exactly with a side of the business. A particular customer or set of customers may be critical for sparking and stoking growth. Catalysts often compete for these "marquee" customers by offering them concessions in return for exclusivity (see the box "The Catalyst's Marquee Strategy"). Sony entered into exclusives for several games, including the hit *Grand Theft Auto*. The contract details aren't known, but Sony likely offered favorable royalty terms in return for these commitments. So Microsoft wasn't able to persuade Rockstar Games to develop an Xbox version of *Grand Theft Auto* for its 2001 console introduction.

Few exclusives are forever, though. Today's exclusive is generally tomorrow's battlefield. Microsoft persuaded Rockstar to make its 2006 release (*Grand Theft Auto: San Andreas*) available for its Xbox 360 console. Asked how this deal came about, Peter Moore, the executive in charge of this Microsoft division, said, coyly, "Well, all I can say is that we're big fans of the franchise. I believe it was instrumental in driving a large part of the installed base of the PlayStation 2. When you look at what's going to drive console adoption, certainly price is always an issue but content and exclusive content are important."[10] Without *Grand Theft* and other exclusive content

The Catalyst's Marquee Strategy

The Nordstrom department store, HBO On Demand, Primary Care, LLC, and Goldman Sachs are all marquee customers. Each has played an important role for catalysts that serve them: they were each the spark that ignited a catalytic reaction and helped get the other side on board.

As we saw in the previous chapter, the prestigious investment banking firm Goldman Sachs occupies ten floors of the Mori Tower in Tokyo's Roppongi Hills. The company not only attracted high-profile retail tenants to this upscale retail and residential mecca, but the investment bank's presence made it attractive for its wealthy employees to live there, which in turn attracted more high-profile residents and tenants. In 2005, Tufts–New England Medical Center finalized a landmark agreement with Primary Care, LLC, as a way to shore up its position in the highly competitive Boston medical marketplace. It's now easier for Tufts to recruit other large physician groups, which in turn bring in patients who in turn bring in more physician groups. Being able to offer HBO On Demand, with its com-

in 2001, Microsoft had to invest significantly in buying up game developers such as Bungie, maker of the hit *Halo* game, and enticing other developers to create content.

The lesson for catalysts:

THE LESSON

For those with a pioneering business model: lock up customers that are essential for a successful reaction to protect your investment. For followers: be prepared to invest significantly in marquee customers and in overcoming exclusive deals by established catalysts.

Catalysts should expect competitors to imitate them, as Diners Club and Nintendo quickly learned. Successful strategies are regu-

pelling content lineup, is seen by cable companies as important for keeping subscribers away from satellite systems and emerging competitors such as Internet Protocol television (IPTV) service providers. Finally, the Old Orchard Center, in Skokie, Illinois, was one of the leading shopping destinations in Chicago for many years. It was in decline by the mid-1980s, and a large portion of its space was unused. It used a marquee strategy to rejuvenate itself in the early 1990s. It gave Nordstrom, a popular American department store based in Washington state, incentives to move into a new 200,000-square-foot part of the mall. And it also got Bloomingdale's to anchor another corner of the mall.

But creating a marquee client strategy goes beyond simply identifying the biggest and most famous potential client in your market and then approaching them about getting on board your platform. Big names rarely come cheap. Value propositions for all sides must be defined, modeled, redefined and remodeled. And the subsidies that often accompany these deals must ultimately enhance profits by getting the right people on board to help grow a profitable catalyst community.

larly imitated by enterprises that think they can execute them better. The fast-food restaurant that starts offering salads and attracts numerous diet-minded customers will soon find that its competitors are also buying more lettuce. Multisided businesses, however, often force firms that serve just one side to transform themselves into catalysts. That's especially so when the profitable multisided business model involves making losses on a side on which the single and multisided firms overlap. All the console makers had to follow Nintendo when it introduced the two-sided models and started subsidizing the distribution of consoles with royalty revenues from game makers.

The magazine industry flipped from being a single-sided to a two-sided industry around the turn of the twentieth century. Most magazines didn't have much advertising in the late nineteenth century. They earned most of their profits from subscription fees. Charles McClure changed that by slashing his subscription fees, creating mass-market magazines, and recovering the lost profits through advertising. His *McClure's Magazine* was the first truly advertising-supported magazine in the United States. His major competitor, Frank Munsey, quickly followed suit. Frank Munsey reduced the cost of his magazine to 10 cents from 25 cents in 1893, believing he could generate more revenue from advertisers. Munsey also realized that by lowering his cover price, he could reach a larger and less affluent audience that previously couldn't afford magazines. It worked. In 1893, the circulation of *Munsey's* was forty thousand; in 1895, it had increased to five hundred thousand.[11] Munsey, more so than McClure, was relentless in seeking a profit from this new catalyst model and is often given credit as the founder of the modern magazine publishing industry. Most everyone had to adopt the same model to compete with the now much cheaper magazine subscriptions.

The lesson for catalysts: there will be an advantage in disrupting a single-sided industry with a two-sided model. But these single-sided platforms—especially the ones now facing money-losing prices for their primary products—will soon realize that they have a choice of copying or folding.

American Express is one of the world's most famous brands, while Diners Club may become a trivia question in a few years. That's in part because the pioneering catalyst did a poor job of protecting itself from imitators, while the imitator excelled—eventually—at using marquee and pricing strategies.

Task 4: Align Interests Internally and Externally

These days, having effective teams whose interests are aligned is critical to success in most businesses. Typically, all team members work for the same firm. But for a catalyst, whose business depends on the participation of different communities outside the company, critical team members often work for complementors—producers of important complementary products. Game developers, even those not owned by Sony, are vital to the PlayStation's success. Because the value of a catalyst to one group is so dependent on another group's attraction to the catalyst, the catalyst entrepreneur must be constantly concerned with aligning interests and incentives both within her firm and within its broader catalyst community. This is a vital part of any profitability plan. A successful catalyst reaches profitability by making sure that every member of its broader team has a compelling interest in actions that help advance the catalyst's profitability.

Internally, that sometimes means setting up divisions that correspond to each key customer group and making sure the head of that division is pursuing the right goal. Microsoft initially intended Xbox's console manufacturing division to be a profit center. The division management, quite understandably, wanted to make money from selling consoles. But as we have observed, the video game business doesn't work that way. Game developers will only invest in games if they are confident that lots of households will have consoles that could play those games. Microsoft soon found that once game developers learned the price point at which it was planning to offer this new console, they had little interest in writing games for it.

Microsoft didn't just have a pricing problem. It had an organizational problem, a problem of misaligned incentives. Key employees didn't have incentives that were aligned with a successful two-sided strategy. The solution: Microsoft kept manufacturing as a separate division but rewarded it based on achieving cost and distribution targets. The decision of how to price the console was taken away from the manufacturing division. The Xbox top managers instead decided on the console price and the extent to which the company would sacrifice operating profit on the consoles. Given this price, the manufacturing arm was rewarded on the basis of producing the consoles at the lowest cost and getting them into the hands of as many people as possible.

THE LESSON

Don't separate a catalyst business by its two sides or try to manage each side by a standard profit and loss statement; the two-sided strategy should drive organization and incentives.

As in the Xbox case, a catalyst manager needs a set of metrics for measuring internal success. Establishing performance metrics has become standard operating procedure in most traditional businesses. In a catalyst business, the issues are slightly different. Many of the activities that ultimately ensure overall profitability lose money when considered narrowly. So the performance metrics must be tied to achieving those goals that drive ultimate profitability—such as securing more participants on the platform or getting them to interact more. Because many of these activities generate out-of-pocket losses, business plans must impose some limits on the losses that can be incurred to achieve broader objectives—too much success, purchased too dearly, can be a very bad thing indeed.

Several companies we talked to, which requested anonymity on this subject, found that their quest for profits was jeopardized by having internal silos that were motivated to earn profits individually rather than securing profits for the platform overall.

The lesson for catalyst entrepreneurs:

THE LESSON

Make sure your internal team has incentives that are aligned with the activities that will drive profitability of the multisided venture.

Giving groups outside the business a stake in the catalyst's success is another part of aligning interests. As we described in chapter 2, software-based catalysts from Apple to Google have had a team member—an "evangelist"—whose main responsibility is to drum up support among developers for the platform even though developers aren't directly a source of profits. The original barnstorming and cult-creation job has evolved into one of organizing large conferences where developers come to hear about all the great new features in the next release of the platform, and the platform's architects find out what developers want. Google appointed Internet pioneer Vinton Cerf as its chief Internet evangelist in 2005. Cerf did not directly contribute to the profit of the Internet search engine; nearly all of that came from online ad sales. But by promoting Google as the best platform for Internet search, Cerf was aligning the interests of software engineers, advertisers, and ultimately innovators who might develop applications for the Google platform.

Creating a path to profitability requires first identifying the group or groups that need to be prompted, cajoled, and persuaded to maintain involvement in the catalyst. Assigning people to maintain relationships with those in each group is another essential part of planning for profit. Microsoft, for example, assigned three representatives to communicate with the Xbox community that used teamxbox.com and other Web sites that attracted Xbox users. The company also sponsors gamer communities such as BioWare, which had more than 2 million members as of 2006.

Because a catalyst business has, by its nature, several groups with different interests, aligning those interests becomes a necessary part of driving the business toward achieving profitability. Those focusing on this objective should heed the following lessons:

THE LESSONS

Identify core responsibilities for achieving profitability. Those responsibilities include securing each group necessary for the reaction and promoting interactions between members of those communities directly or indirectly.

Identify metrics that measure success in helping to ignite and sustain the catalytic reaction. For loss-making sides, those metrics will often involve targets for the number of members of the group who sign up or the number of interactions they engage in.

The Profitability Path and the Catalyst Framework

By the time Microsoft entered the video game market, the catalyst model was already well established. Nintendo, Sony, and others had already figured out the chicken-and-egg problem that stymies most start-up catalyst businesses. Having achieved the ability to attract different groups around a single platform, the catalyst entrepreneur then has to ask the next set of questions: will the positive feedbacks that one group generates for another remain strong? Do the losses I need to incur in attracting one side of the marketplace prevent me from realizing an overall profit in a reasonable period of time? Will moves by competitors upset the catalytic balance I have achieved? Can I anticipate the impact of new entrants in the market?

Answering these types of questions early in the business formation process is what it means to create a profitability road map—and complete this element within the catalyst framework (see table 6-1). Because creating the initial catalytic reaction between two or more sides of market can be so hard to get right, simply achieving the network effect that catalysts create is easily mistaken for the most important business achievement. But catalyst businesses, like any other, have to meet all the demands of a changing marketplace. Careful analysis of profitability forces the entrepreneur to test whether the cat-

TABLE 6-1

Mapping a profitability road map

Tasks	Lessons
Study industry history.	• Understand what worked—and what didn't—for business predecessors. • Don't assume that what worked as a catalyst in a related industry will work as well for your business.
Use forecasts to enhance profitability.	• Make realistic forecasts about losses. Evaluate the risks. • Make sure catalytic reaction can be sustained for long-term profit. Know when to cut and run.
Anticipate competitors' actions.	• Pioneers: lock up customers that are essential for a successful reaction. • Followers: be prepared to invest significantly in marquee customers.
Align interests internally and externally.	• Don't manage each side of the business separately. • Offer incentives to your internal team that drive overall profitability, not divisional success. • Identify core responsibilities for profitability. • Identify metrics that develop and sustain the catalytic reaction.

alytic reaction he has triggered is merely an interesting economic relationship among different players or a real, sustainable business.

Microsoft's experience shows that even the best-executed strategy for entering an established multisided business in no guarantee of financial rewards. The Xbox team got many things exactly right. They learned from history. They veered away from challenging the two-sided models that had proved so successful, and copied the approach that fueled the growth of Nintendo and Sony. They got prices right and worked their way around Sony's lock on game distributors. The Xbox was a hit among those who play games and those who make games. Yet, despite the fact that the Xbox was created by the developer of perhaps the most profitable catalyst business of all time—the Windows software platform—it has not met Microsoft's original profit forecasts and, while an important strategic asset, does not appear poised to reverse its operating losses. But as the experience of American Express shows, catalysts can quickly move from an unprofitable to a profitable path as a result of scale and positive feedback effects. A stumble by Sony during the Christmas 2006 season (a poorly received console or one with software or hardware bugs) or a huge hit from an exclusive game maker for the Xbox could turn what now looks like a dubious investment into an enormously profitable one.

Whether Microsoft achieves profitability or not, its aggressive entry is also a reminder that even businesses that seem strongly rooted atop their industry—in this case, Nintendo, Sony, and Atari—can expect challenges from unlikely quarters. This is a recurring challenge for catalyst businesses. In the next chapter, we will examine it in more detail as we see how some traditional catalysts have seen the Internet open the doors to new catalytic challengers.

7

Compete Strategically with
Other Catalysts

Every wall is a door.

—Ralph Waldo Emerson

It is the winter of 2003. A customer with fourteen thousand desktop computers wouldn't ordinarily get the attention of Steve Ballmer, president and CEO of Microsoft, which licenses its Windows software to almost every significant businesses, government agency, and educational institution in the world. He certainly wouldn't lose sleep over an order that would amount to about $36 million—about a third of 1 percent of Microsoft's annual revenue from its standard Windows operating system in fiscal year 2003.[1] But this customer, the City of Munich, the capital of Bavaria and the third-largest city in Germany, was seriously considering switching from Microsoft's Windows and Office software to competing software that is built and constantly improved by volunteers working over the Internet—open source software or, as it is sometimes known, *software libre*. Microsoft executives knew that losing this small battle could cost them dearly in the war that the open source movement was waging against the software giant worldwide.

Some say Ballmer rushed from the ski slops to meet with the city's mayor. Others say he was on a scheduled business trip to Germany. Either way, Ballmer spent forty-five minutes personally pitching Munich's mayor on Microsoft's competing proposal. And to win the business, Microsoft offered dramatic price reductions, free consulting services, and other concessions. To no avail, though: on May 28, 2003, the Munich City Council voted 50 to 30 in favor of switching the city's software to open source products—the Linux operating system and the OpenOffice suite of office productivity applications.

Of course, software libre—like the proverbial free lunch—isn't really free. Microsoft lost to two companies that were just as interested in making money as it was. IBM had teamed with Munich-based SuSE Linux to offer conveniently assembled open source software packages and to provide consulting services to make them work. They initially came in with a price that was slightly higher than Microsoft's opening bid, and by the end their offer was far higher than Microsoft's. The city council went with open source not because it was free, or even cheaper, but because it believed open source was the future and that relying on this constantly changing group of volunteers, working around the globe over the Internet, gave it more control than relying on Microsoft.

Ideology played a role in Munich's decision. Software libre seemed philosophically aligned with other anticapitalist movements in vogue in Europe, such as the proenvironment Green Party. Moreover, Germans were proud of SuSE Linux and other German companies that were creating a homegrown software industry based on open source. But when it comes to booting your computer up every morning, ideology and politics only go so far. The Münchners would not have been able to reject Microsoft's ever more attractive offers if the competing open source software hadn't been quite good.

Microsoft versus open source is one of the great catalyst clashes in the first few years of the twenty-first century. It also reminds us that even the most successful catalysts are not immune from competitive threats. Indeed, the clash of catalysts—new catalysts taking on existing ones—will be a common feature in the future economic landscape. Table 7-1 shows several examples of catalyst clashes at the beginning of the twenty-first century.

Preparing for competition—and understanding where it might come from—forms another element in the catalyst framework, shown in figure 7-1. In this chapter, we examine in more detail the special characteristics of the competition that catalyst businesses face. We also look at how catalyst competition is taking shape in different types of business, such as online search, mobile communications, and retail. We will see that performing the following tasks reveals tactics entrepreneurs can use to challenge the entrenched catalysts of today, along with lessons that can help a successful catalyst defend against emerging threats.

1. **Understand the dynamics of catalyst competition.** Multihoming and intersecting catalysts are two unique and important aspects of competition among catalysts. They

TABLE 7-1

Twenty-first century catalyst clashes

Industry	The old	The new	Example
Software platforms	Proprietary firms	Linux	Microsoft Windows versus open source Linux
Retailing	Shopping malls	E-tailers	Waterstone's books versus Amazon.com
Advertising	Newspapers, magazines, free television	Internet search engines	*Chicago Sun Times* versus craigslist Chicago; CBS TV versus Google
Payments	General-purpose payment cards	Mobile phone–enabled payments	JCB Card versus i-mode
Travel services	Travel agents	Internet-based travel	Thomas Cooke Travel versus Orbitz
Radio	Terrestrial radio	Satellite radio, Internet-based radio	Clear Channel versus RealNetworks's Rhapsody

FIGURE 7-1

The catalyst framework: compete strategically with other catalysts

Identify the platform community	Establish a pricing structure	Design the catalyst for success	Focus on profitability	Compete strategically with other catalysts	Experiment and evolve
• Identify distinct groups that need each other	• Set separate prices for access and usage	• Attract multiple customer groups that need each other	• Study industry history	• Understand the dynamics of catalyst competition	• Know when to be first—and when to follow
• Determine why and how much they need each other	• Set prices to balance demand from two sides	• Promote interactions	• Use forecasts to enhance profitability	• Look for competition from different business models	• Control growth
• Evaluate who else is serving the community	• Price to grow slowly—at first	• Minimize transaction costs	• Anticipate competitor actions		• Protect your back
• Compare a multisided business model with a single-sided one	• Pay customers to belong—sometimes	• Design for evolution	• Align interests internally and externally	• Leverage to attack	• Plan for what's next
	• Price for long-term profits			• Consider cooperation	• Look out for the cops
Find out who needs whom— and why	**Shape participation and maximize profits**	**Draw customers and facilitate interactions**	**Visualize path toward long-term profit**	**Challenge existing catalysts and react to new catalyst threats**	**Pursue evolutionary strategy for growth**

shape both the threats that catalysts face from one another and the opportunities for new entrants in a market dominated by catalysts.

2. **Look for competition from different business models.** Catalysts frequently face competition not from imitators but from innovators, which may offer a substantially different product or a similar product developed and distributed using a different business model.

3. **Leverage to attack.** Attack an entrenched catalyst in one industry from an entrenched catalyst position in another industry. Use the community built up in one industry to

add features and services that can challenge rivals in another industry.

4. **Consider cooperation.** In some cases, evolving technology will create new opportunities—or new threats—where there are overlapping catalysts. It will sometimes be better for an established catalyst to cooperate with a new catalyst than to attack it.

Task 1: Understand the Dynamics of Catalyst Competition

ABC, CBS, and NBC—the three television networks that broadcast, over the air, the evening programming watched in most U.S. households for almost half a century—have seen how quickly catalysts can lose their hard-won customers. Their share of viewers between the ages of eighteen and forty-nine—the ones most coveted by the advertisers that provide all their revenues— dropped from 31.3 percent to 30.2 percent in 2004 alone.[2] Figure 7-2 shows the trend in viewership for the networks.

Many of these viewers watch other networks made possible by cable television, DVDs, or something they've downloaded on their computers. The younger ones, especially, play games on their video consoles, surf the Internet, and, even when they are watching, are often distracted with e-mailing or instant messaging their friends or fidgeting with their other gadgets.

Just as viewers have more alternatives for getting content, advertisers have more alternatives for reaching the right eyeballs and ears. Advertisers that want to reach Gen Y—the 56 million Americans born between 1977 and 1990—promote everything from Internet access services to tax preparation, free smiley face downloads, and dating services on MySpace.com. They can also figure out the kind of Internet searches that their most likely customers might conduct, and pay advertising-supported search engines, such as Google and Yahoo!, for space on the pages that report these searches.

FIGURE 7-2

Comparative prime-time ratings for Big Three broadcast networks (ABC, NBC, and CBS), 1997–2006

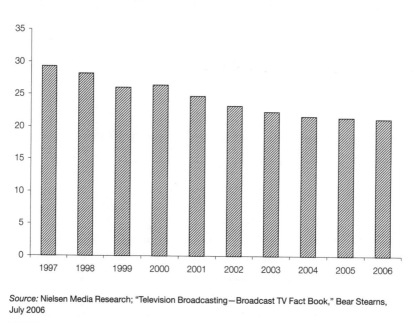

Source: Nielsen Media Research; "Television Broadcasting—Broadcast TV Fact Book," Bear Stearns, July 2006

ABC, CBS, and NBC are facing stiffer competition from many quarters. Their travails illustrate two powerful concepts for understanding the dynamics of competition in two-sided businesses: multihoming and intersecting catalysts.

Multihoming

Multihoming occurs when customers use two or more competing catalysts at the same time. (Single-homing occurs when they use just one provider.) That's the case with the broadcast networks, as shown in figure 7-3. Advertisers and viewers are polygamists. Similarly, most merchants accept several payment card brands, and many consumers carry and use several different cards. Computer operating system vendors usually face multihoming only on one side. It isn't practical—or in some cases even possible—for people

FIGURE 7-3

Multihoming and network television

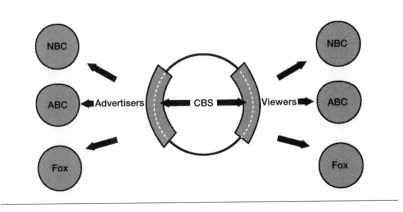

to use more than one operating system on their personal computers, video game consoles, or mobile phones. Many developers,
though, write programs or games for several operating systems. Roke
Manor Research, Ltd., for instance, a Siemens company in the United
Kingdom, develops applications for a variety of mobile phone platforms, including Symbian, Pocket PC, and Palm OS.

If you want to build or invest in a catalyst, you must care about
multihoming.

Customers often make two sequential decisions when it comes
to relying on multisided businesses. Should I join the "club"? And
how often should I use the "club"? Once they've joined the club—
and most catalysts make this easy with low access fees—it is very
natural to use it. If, however, they've joined several catalysts, then
it is quite easy for them to switch usage between them. Cardholders
can pull their Amex cards from their wallets just as easily as their
Visa cards. Television viewers can switch from CBS to the Discovery Channel with a flick of the remote. Multihoming reduces the
stickiness that many single-sided companies can count on to maintain customer loyalty.

Multihoming is important for another reason: it reduces the force
of positive feedbacks. Catalysts grow by getting more customers on
one side to attract more customers on the other side. These attractive

forces are much weaker if customers on either side can get access to the customers on the other side through another catalyst.

Understanding multihoming leads to two lessons for catalysts:

THE LESSONS

Catalysts, particularly market leaders, should limit customer multihoming through product design. Later we will see that eBay has used its Feedback Forum to make buyers and sellers very loyal to eBay. They lose the "reputational capital" that has accumulated on eBay if they use another auction site.

Catalysts should recognize that customers who multihome are highly sensitive to the value proposition, and therefore make sure they have a compelling value proposition for those customers. When there is multihoming on only one side, the practical implication of this lesson is to be particularly cautious about raising prices on that side.

Intersecting Catalysts

Catalysts most commonly face competition from multisided businesses that serve the same customers as they do. These *overlapping catalysts* often have comparable business models. They often adopt similar pricing policies. ABC, CBS, NBC, and Fox TV in the United States all serve viewers and advertisers, doing so in broadly similar ways, and make their profits from advertisers, as shown in figure 7-4.

Catalysts sometimes face competition from single-sided businesses. Network television faced one of its biggest threats from TiVo when it was first introduced. TiVo began life as a box with a hard drive that was capable of not only time-shifting content but skipping the ads that generated all the networks' revenues. Although TiVo has evolved into a catalyst with its own ad-supported capabilities, it created more than a little nervousness on the part of television advertisers and content creators alike that feared that their revenue streams would essentially evaporate.

Competition from *intersecting catalysts* can be trickier still. Suppose catalyst 1 decides to offer a below-cost price to customer

FIGURE 7-4

Overlapping catalysts

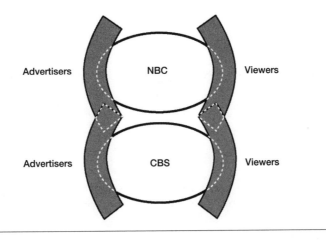

group A and earn its profits from customer group B. Catalyst 2 then appears to serves customer groups B and C. Catalyst 2 decides to offer a below-cost price to side B and earn its profits from side C. If both catalysts are providing a similar service to side B, the business model adopted by catalyst 1 doesn't work anymore: it won't be able to price above catalyst 2 to group B and therefore won't be able to subsidize group A. Catalyst 1 can survive only if it can differentiate its product to customer group B.

For instance, as we noted earlier, local newspapers charge for all classified ads and provide them to readers (as part of a larger bundle) at prices that just cover printing and distribution costs, while in some areas craigslist lets consumers list and browse for free and charges only employers (see figure 7-5).

A recent study shows that craigslist shifted some $50 million to $65 million a year (including help-wanted ads) away from newspapers in the San Francisco Bay Area alone in 2004.[3] Newspapers have responded with a variety of online offerings.

As this example indicates, the need to lose money to one group is a real source of vulnerability for catalysts, since it requires earning all profits from the other group. That's fine as long as they are competing with other catalysts with the same model. But it can be fatal when they collide with businesses that offer the profit-generating

FIGURE 7-5

Intersecting catalysts and newspaper classified advertising

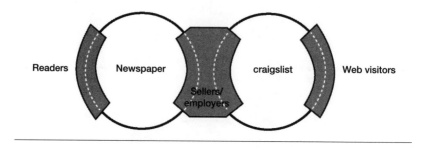

customers a better deal. This provides catalysts with several lessons
for surveying the competitive landscape for threats:

THE LESSONS

Watch what overlapping competing catalysts are doing. Just
as in a single-sided business, you need to watch how your direct competitors are adjusting their prices and product offerings. But remember—changes in relative prices and products
get magnified through positive feedback. Little changes can
have a big impact.

Watch out for intersecting catalysts. See whether other catalysts are providing a similar service to one of your groups of
customers. You need to pay very close attention to how their
prices compare with yours and whether their business model
is incompatible with yours. If your low-margin side is their
high-margin side, they have to worry. Otherwise, you do. Survival then probably depends on strongly differentiating your
offering from theirs.

Watch out for single-sided competitors. Identify firms that
aren't catalysts but are providing a competing service to one of
your customer groups. If they are competing on your low-margin
side, you are likely to destroy them. But if they are competing on
your high-margin side, you are vulnerable. As with an intersecting catalyst, differentiation may be the only road to survival.

Task 2: Look for Competition from
Different Business Models

Richard Stallman looks like a homeless man who sleeps on park benches and carries his clothes in a plastic sack. He has long, unkempt black hair and beard and seems unwashed. And he can sound like a street preacher seeking converts and railing against the evils of the world. He is also the genius who started the catalytic reaction that brought Steve Ballmer to Munich.

Stallman didn't come up with a new product like the general-purpose payment card or a new business model like advertising-supported radio. He didn't even have any interest in making money. Instead, in 1985, he came up with a contract—a legally binding agreement that relied on copyright laws—that started a catalytic reaction among software programmers and users around the world.

In the early days of computers, companies like IBM made their money from hardware. Most software was custom-built by individual users for particular tasks. There was no market for software. Programmers shared blocks of code because they got some recognition, helped their friends, and weren't losing any money by doing so. Hardware companies also made some software available for free because it helped stimulate hardware sales. A market for software eventually developed, and it grew rapidly after personal computers became popular. Software companies distributed their products in a form that computers understood—a string of 0s and 1s called *object code*—but other programmers couldn't readily decode.

Stallman thought it was immoral to charge for software and thought it should be distributed as human-readable *source code* rather than unintelligible bits. He started the Free Software Foundation to pursue his vision of a software utopia that wasn't infected by greed. He recognized, though, that people wouldn't cooperate with each other if others could take the fruits of their efforts without giving anything in return.

The General Public License (GPL) was his brilliant solution to this problem. If you make a software program you have written available as source code to others under the condition that they comply with the GPL, those recipients must distribute any revision they make to your program under the GPL as well. Thus any improvements to your program are returned to the community—and beyond, since those outside the community of contributors also get the benefits.

The GPL helped fuel a catalytic reaction among programmers who wanted to write useful code and end users who wanted to use software to help solve problems. The GPL is by far the most popular license in what is called the open source movement. As of November 2006, over twenty-nine thousand projects were being developed under this license.[4] Popular programs that use the GPL are widely distributed. For example, MySQL, which is a database program that competes with Oracle Database, is installed on more than 4 million computers.[5]

Linux—the Windows alternative—is one of the best-known products of the open source movement. Linus Torvalds wrote the first version of this operating system by building on code that Stallman's group had written and released under the GPL. Torvalds posted his version on the Web. Soon programmers around the world were making contributions. He periodically reviewed these contributions—some were corrections of bugs, others were additions—and released new official versions of Linux that incorporated worthwhile suggestions. Now known as the "Benevolent Dictator for Life," Torvalds oversees Linux, which is installed on about 11 percent of the servers that organizations use for managing their networks, handling their Web sites, and running large applications.[6]

Today, Linux is a big business, with companies such as IBM paying many "volunteers" to help improve the source code. But that shouldn't make us lose sight of the fact that a group of individuals working over the Internet, lightly managed by Torvalds and a few others, have written 5.7 million lines of code that Google uses to run its vast array of servers, that Digital Domain used to create the special effects for the movie *Titanic*, that thousands of sophisticated businesses around the world use daily, and that has proved to be one of the most significant threats to Microsoft's profit stream.

Thus, Ballmer rushed to Munich for good reasons. Open source doesn't just produce good software. It is based on a business model that clashes with the model followed by Microsoft, Symbian, Apple, and others that make software platforms for profit.

Microsoft invests enormous amounts of money in writing code for its Windows software platform. Following a two-sided pricing strategy, it largely gives away the services of this platform to developers and earns profits from licensing its software to computer users and computer makers, which in turn make it available to computer users. The open source community gives its product away to *both* sides. That makes Linux and other open source software tough competitors for price-conscious customers, including governments in developing countries. The "for-free" model also explains the enthusiasm that IBM and other hardware companies have for Linux. Their customers want hardware and software platforms. They can get a bigger profit on their hardware if they, or their customers, can get a cheaper software platform. (Or if, as in the case of Munich, the "social" benefits of open source outweigh the advantages of the Windows-based alternative.)

This Linux community stayed under most radar for many years. But in 2005, fourteen years after Torvalds posted the first Linux code, a *Business Week* cover story announced, "Linux, Inc.: Linus Torvalds once led a ragtag band of software geeks. Not anymore. Here's an inside look at how the unusual Linux business model increasingly threatens Microsoft."[7]

The competition between Microsoft and open source software provides lessons for both existing catalysts facing a threat and for the company that wants to take on the incumbent players. For incumbents like Microsoft, these are the lessons:

THE LESSONS

Look for competition in unexpected places. Catalysts should always keep an eye out for other catalysts with different business models—because these are often the most dangerous and lead to the most brutal clashes. Microsoft was caught off guard when price-conscious companies and governments started switching to the seemingly cheaper alternative, and reacted only after software libre had gained considerable momentum.

Pay close attention to any business or technology that provides or can provide value to members of your catalyst communities. The danger is particularly acute when competitors
have a different source of profits than you or when they have a
technological advantage over you. The competition between
Microsoft and open source is at bottom a battle between business models with very different cost and pricing structures.

For new entrants, the lesson is different:

THE LESSON

Innovate rather than imitate is the secret to challenging an
established catalyst. The open source innovation wasn't in the
software but in the institutions for coordinating thousands of
independent programmers around the world and in the contracts—the GPL, in particular—for solving the free-rider
problem. The Free Software Foundation succeeded because,
unlike other Microsoft competitors, it didn't try to tackle
Microsoft head-on.

Task 3: Leverage to Attack

New competition also sneaked up on the newspaper industry. But
it now poses a mortal danger. Between 2003 and 2006, as shown
in figure 7-6, the market capitalization of each of the ten largest
American newspaper companies declined, by 40 percent overall,
wiping out $32 billion of value even though the major stock in-
dexes were rising.[8]

Web-based competitors have significantly disrupted the newspapers' advertising-based business model in three ways. The value of
newspaper content to readers declined because consumers could get
much of it on the Web—and they could get it whenever they wanted
it. Moreover, Web-based advertising reduced the value of newspapers as a vehicle for displaying ads, especially classified advertising.

The third source of disruption is the most interesting. Instead
of providing prepackaged content to attract viewers for advertise-

FIGURE 7-6

Decline in newspaper market capitalization, 2003–2006

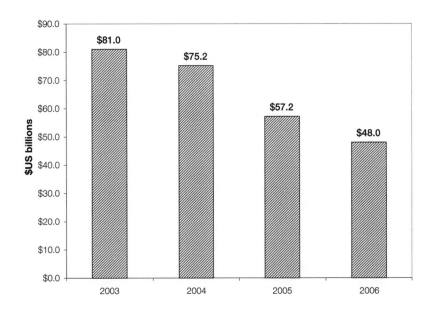

Source: Market capitalization data for 2003–2005 from Bloomberg 2006; data for 2006 as of August 24, 2006, according to Yahoo! Finance

Note: Data represents the market capitalization of the top 10 newspaper companies, as ranked by Yahoo! Finance, as of August 24, 2006.

ments, these young catalysts—Google and Yahoo! being the biggest and most famous—had search engines that attracted consumers who were looking for things on the World Wide Web. In addition, they had devised a way to charge advertisers according to whether consumers "clicked through" the advertisements presented to them. Advertisers knew that they had made a connection with a consumer who clicked through, whereas they didn't know they had made a connection with a reader who bought a newspaper in which they had placed an ad. The search engines provided a value that printed newspapers couldn't match.

Thus, print newspapers—and in fact all traditional advertising-supported catalysts—face a new competitor that is mounting a frontal assault, with lots of eyeballs and a more effective way of connecting those eyeballs to advertisers. The advertising-supported search engines have the same business model and earn profits from the same side (advertisers), and subsidize the same side (viewers) as traditional advertisers. They are what we have called an "overlapping catalyst" when it comes to newspapers, magazines, and television.

Traditional media were caught by surprise. Some *leveraged to protect* by building Web portals. The *Wall Street Journal* has been the most successful. It was able to establish a subscription-based Web site early on. As a leading provider of valuable financial reporting, it was able to get people to pay for timely access to news. Moreover, because it didn't rely on classifieds, its advertising revenue was less vulnerable to Web-based competition. And advertisers found the Web site a valuable adjunct for reaching the *Journal*'s upscale audience.

The *New York Times* has also managed to shore up its position. Like most other newspaper dot-coms, it found that subscription fees drove people away from its Web site. But as Web-based advertising became more popular, the roughly 1.5 million people who came to nytimes.com each day by 2006 were a valuable set of eyeballs.[9] Still, the effectiveness of this counterstrategy is limited in this case. The search engines can easily identify people who are likely to want a particular product or service. A browser who searches for a tagine is probably also interested in buying Moroccan cookware. Most traditional media can't sort consumers like that even with a Web site—they are much better at delivering largely undifferentiated eyeballs. This approach may work better for magazines that have proved to be effective catalysts for bringing together niche communities of readers and advertisers, as we saw with Japanese men's magazine *Leon*, described in chapter 5.

Accentuate the positive is probably a better strategy here. Catalysts that can't withstand a frontal assault should emphasize features that differentiate them. Traditional media catalysts are better vehicles than search engine–based catalysts for broadcasting repetitious messages to large audiences. They continue to have an edge for companies that want to build a brand name, or that benefit from large numbers of eyeballs because most people consume their kind of product or service. National television networks and newspapers have the best chance of surviving by focusing on these advantages. Local television stations and metropolitan newspapers face a more difficult problem. They lack the razorlike focus of certain magazines on the one hand and the reach of national media on the other hand. (The rise of suburban and neighborhood papers, like the *Cambridge Chronicle* and *Beacon Hill Times* in the Boston area, reflects in part the value of focus to advertisers.)

Another strategy for survival in the face of a catalyst collision is to *revise pricing and design*. At least one significant customer group values the traditional catalyst less because they now have a new catalyst as an alternative. The traditional catalyst will almost certainly take a profit hit. The challenge is minimizing the loss of profits and preventing wholesale destruction. Most traditional advertising-supported media were not proactive in following this lesson. Over time, more are likely to find that they have to increase the price to readers as their advertising revenue declines, and some may go back to the very old days when newspapers and magazines were largely one-sided businesses financed through subscriptions.

The advertising-supported search engines are also mounting lateral attacks on other industries by subsidizing a side from which other catalysts earn profits. They are "intersecting catalysts" in these battles: they can make products and services available for free so long as they have enough advertising revenue coming in to offset the investment cost. Google, especially, is a force of disruptive change that instills fear in the hearts and boardrooms of many mature catalysts as well as single-sided businesses.

Larry Page and Sergey Brin started Google with an innovative software program for constructing and updating an index of the World Wide Web. Armed with this software and a massive amount of computing power, they begged and borrowed, and beginning in 1998, Google was able to deliver search results that Web users found more relevant than those delivered by other portals. Page and Brin then started selling advertising using the pay-per-click approach, as we discussed in chapter 2. They had, perhaps inadvertently, launched a software platform that could bring diverse communities together and provide value to them that was previously unattainable. And they started a catalytic reaction of gargantuan proportion. Google's advertising revenue reached $6.1 billion in 2005, more than the New York Times Company and Dow Jones & Company combined.[10] There were nearly 2.5 billion Google searches in December 2005 from within the United States alone, which led to 16.5 trillion click-throughs in the United States to paid advertisers.[11]

Google sees profits whenever it can figure out a way to deliver advertising to customers. That's what keeps businesspeople in many industries awake at night. Microsoft's desktop franchise is one target. For Microsoft, the computer screen is the place where computer users interact with its software platform and where it can help them organize their applications. For Google, the computer screen is valuable real estate where it can place advertising directly or programs that take people to pages that have advertising. It is therefore developing various software programs and giving them away for free in the apparent hopes that this will increase its advertising opportunities. It is also providing free software services to developers. In exchange, those developers have to agree to let Google place advertisements on their applications when they run. One can imagine Google subsidizing the development of Linux-based personal computers with the advertising revenue it can earn from the desktop.

Google Maps, for example, is a program that helps people conveniently find locations on their personal computers and mobile devices. Google has made it available to software developers that are creating a variety of applications such as identifying pockets of crime or finding restaurants. The search engine behemoth is using a classic *leverage to attack* strategy by using the catalyst communities it has developed to move into adjacent markets where it can extend its advertising-supported model.

Google's rivals were caught off guard by the company's explosive growth. Most have turned belatedly to *leverage to protect* and *imitate to survive* counterstrategies. Unlike the traditional media firms that lacked the technical competence to pursue these tactics, tech-savvy firms such as Yahoo! and Microsoft have it in abundance. They are investing in search engine technologies in an attempt to leapfrog Google's offering and in developing imitative advertising-supported ventures. Meanwhile, Page and Brin are investing in improving their search and advertising technologies, racing to stay ahead. They are also encouraging developers to write applications and consumers to use those applications—a classic strategy followed by all software platforms to create an ecosystem that is dependent on, and thus bound to, the platform.

The same phenomenon can also be seen in the retail sector. A decade after it started, eBay had almost 180 million registered users who exchanged more than $44.3 billion worth of goods.[12] Some of these goods would never have been sold without an auction-based e-tailer like eBay. They would have just languished in someone's attic or in the back room of a small shop, or been dumped in the trash. Increasingly, though, many of eBay's goods are sold in competition with existing retailers. This new catalyst—along with Alibaba in China, Yahoo! Japan, and a host of other, smaller e-tailers—is behind a revolution that is disrupting the full breadth of the retail industry.

EBay Motors provides one example of how this Web portal is colliding with traditional retailers. Nearly $14 billion worth of cars and trucks were sold by eBay in 2005.[13] Some of these vehicles were bought and sold by individuals who would have relied on a car dealer if eBay hadn't made it so easy for them. Dealers still survive, but they are under more competitive pressure than ever before.

As with many other new catalysts, a software platform is a key source of eBay's power. This platform has grown from a few lines of code running on Pierre Omidyar's home computer in 1995 to more than 6 million lines running on nine thousand server computers in 2005.[14] This code provides the increasing number of features that eBay makes available to buyers and sellers to make their transactions more convenient. Writing code that is efficient and bug free requires deep expertise and hard work. But it is much easier to expand by using good code more intensively on more computers than by building more factories or retail outlets.

Originally, eBay's software platform brought buyers and sellers together. By 2000 eBay decided to bring in another community: software developers that could write applications that eBay's buyers and sellers could use to increase the value they obtain from eBay. It provided developers with access to the software platform, provided them with tools for writing programs, developed a laboratory for testing their programs, and offered a prize for the best application. By 2005, eBay had more than twenty-one thousand developers registered with its program. They had written sixteen hundred applications for buyers and sellers.[15]

The e-tailers, from Alibaba to Yahoo!, have been *leveraging to attack* much of the retail industry. They began initially helping people trade the sorts of things that are advertised in the classified advertisements in newspapers or sold at bazaars or in suburban American garage sales. After building up this core strength in person-to-person transactions, these e-tailers moved to business-to-consumer and business-to-business transactions.

In response, some traditional retailers have *leveraged to protect*. They have started their own e-tailing sites. Wal-Mart sold more than $1 billion worth of goods through Walmart.com in 2005. That's less than 1 percent of Wal-Mart's overall sales that year of $290 billion, but it is sure to grow.[16] That is a plausible counterstrategy for many of the large retailers. Others have *cooperated to survive*. They have recognized that eBay has something to offer that they can't match. They have developed virtual stores on eBay and are using tools provided by eBay and the developer community to increase their sales. Retailers such as Summit Racing Equipment, Today's Designer, and National Music Supply are playing the eBay game of low prices and high customer satisfaction. Many retailers, though, will find that they can't survive in the e-tailing world.

The basic lesson for catalysts:

THE LESSON

Watch out for new technologies that can provide a better way to serve your communities; embrace these technologies before they destroy you. In either attacking or defensive modes, consider first strategies that leverage your strengths.

Task 4: Consider Cooperation

Along with billions of other people around the world, you probably carry both a mobile phone and one or more payment cards.

These two devices will star either in one of the greatest catalyst clashes of the next few years or in one of the grandest catalyst marriages. The players in this game face a question that many catalysts will face in the years to come: should they attack or should they cooperate to survive?

Most people in the United States still have dumb payment cards with just a magnetic stripe on the back. As we noted in chapter 5, however, the card industry is pushing both smart cards, in which the stripe is replaced by a computer chip, and contactless cards, which can be read when waved by a special reader. Despite the obstacles we discussed, Frost & Sullivan predict that 30 percent of payment cards issued globally by 2009 will be smart cards. [17] It will be possible to store and retrieve information from smart cards and, at least in principle, to load and run applications on these computing devices.

As a payment device, however, the mobile phone has several advantages over smart payment cards. It is naturally a more powerful computing device as a result of its larger size. It has a keyboard and screen that enable consumers to enter and view information—selecting different card accounts or purchasing things online, for instance. And it can communicate with the Internet so that people can sync up accounts and conduct other financial transactions online. It turns out that it is relatively easy to incorporate the smart-card and contactless technologies right into the mobile phone.

A catalyst clash could result if mobile phone operators *leverage to attack* the payment card industry. In Japan, i-mode is behind this scenario, as we noted in chapter 5. The transactions don't go through any existing payment card system. Instead, subscribers are charged and merchants are reimbursed through i-mode's highly efficient billing system. (Japanese consumers seldom finance purchases with cards. However, i-mode has collaborated with banks to create mobile phone–based credit cards.)

A catalyst marriage could result if payment card systems entered into partnerships with mobile phone operators—if they elected to *cooperate to survive*. Over the last half century, the payment card industry has developed deep experience in credit scoring, fraud detection, and risk management that can make the difference between profits and catastrophic losses. They could incorporate their technologies into mobile phones and gradually replace cards with phones. Mobile phone operators could allow their subscribers to manage several payment cards—and perhaps even their bank accounts—from their mobile phones. Consumers could toggle between these different payment options on their phones just as they now pull out different payment cards from their wallets—or reach for their checkbooks—when they go to pay.

Like the marriage of royals from different countries centuries ago, a joining of payment card systems and mobile operators could align incentives and reduce conflict. However, this would be a marriage fraught with tensions.

The mobile operators would exert significant control over the relationship with consumers. They could use this asset to strike exclusive deals with particular card systems or card issuers. For example, one could imagine Vodafone striking a deal with American Express whereby Vodafone's subscribers could use their phones to pay only with their Amex accounts. The mobile operators could also strike a variety of preferential deals. For example, Vivo's mobile phones might come with an HSBC Bank Brasil MasterCard account already set up, although subscribers would have the choice of loading other competing cards on the phones. A key strategic issue would be whether the mobile operators would really commit to a single payment card partner.

The payment systems would enter the marriage with millions of merchants around the world that accept their card brands. They could use this asset to secure favorable exclusives from the mobile operators. For example, MasterCard could enter into exclusives with mobile operators whose subscribers would then be able to use their phones to pay for things at any MasterCard merchant equipped to take contactless devices.

These colliding catalysts should consider several features of multisided businesses in evaluating whether to attack or, if they cooperate, what kind of deal to negotiate.

First, they earn profits from different sides. The payment systems make their money from merchants, while the mobile operators earn profits from consumers. The mobile operators can use this fact to consider whether they could subsidize the creation of their own merchant acceptance network. That's what i-mode did in Japan. Even the threat of starting their own acceptance network could get them more favorable terms with the payment systems.

Second, they have different competitive strengths. Most mobile phone customers use only one mobile phone operator: they single-home. Subscribers don't readily switch between operators. Most cardholders have several cards: they multihome. Cardholders can readily shift transactions between cards and can readily replace one card with another. Payment card systems could make their customers stickier by entering into exclusives with mobile operators; mobile operators could get a premium by selling their exclusive real estate.

Third, they operate under dissimilar market conditions with different entry barriers. Some countries have a single payment system but several mobile operators. In France, for example, one payment system accounts for most card transactions, but there are several competing mobile operators. Other countries, such as Korea and Japan, have a dominant mobile operator but several competing card systems. And in still other countries, such as the United States, there are several competing mobile operators as well as several competing payment systems. A dominant catalyst protected by natural and legal entry barriers is in a better position to attack or cooperate in name only. In Japan, NTT DoCoMo succeeded in establishing a mobile phone–based payment system in part because it faced a weak payment card industry.

THE LESSON

In deciding whether to attack or cooperate, a catalyst needs to determine which side of the market its competitor's profits come from, to understand whether customers will multihome, and to evaluate barriers to entry.

Competing Strategically and the
Catalyst Framework

Catalysts have been central to economic progress for at least three millennia. They were responsible for the village markets that brought buyers and sellers together and enabled benefits to be generated from the division of labor. They were responsible for the first money, which expanded trade through increasingly large geographic regions. They created institutions like auctions and exchanges that made it easier for buyers and sellers to get together. They spawned the vast use of advertising for conveying information about products and prices. And they've been the source of better and broader communication from the telegraph to the mobile phone and from the mail to mass media.

Historically, long periods have separated the great catalyst innovations. That changed at the end of the twentieth century. New catalysts are born rapid fire. They have propelled the economy into a period of what the great Austrian economist Joseph Schumpeter called "creative destruction." As a result, deciding how to take on an existing catalyst, or how to deal with one that wants to displace you from the market, is a normal and expected part of multisided businesses. That is why we consider it an essential element of the catalyst framework, shown in table 7-2.

Responding to competitive threats, or becoming a competitive threat, helps illustrate how a catalyst evolves during its lifetime. This evolution, and the way a catalyst can extend the scope of its business, is the focus of the next chapter, which describes the final element of the catalyst framework.

TABLE 7-2

Competing strategically with other catalysts

Tasks	Lessons
Understand the dynamics of catalyst competition.	• Watch out for "multihoming" and "intersecting" catalysts and how they shape the competitive landscape.
Look for competition from different business models.	• Look for competition in unexpected places. • Pay attention to any business that can provide value to members of your catalyst communities.
Leverage to attack.	• Watch out for new technologies that can provide a better way to serve your communities. • Embrace technology before it destroys you.
Consider cooperation.	• Determine which side of the market competitors' profits come from. • Understand whether customers will multihome. • Evaluate barriers to entry before deciding whether to cooperate or attack.

8

Experiment and Evolve

It is not the strongest species that survive,

nor the most intelligent, but the ones who are

most responsive to change.

—CHARLES DARWIN

AMERICAN READERS KNOW THAT HOWARD STERN IS THE
"shock jock" of radio and television. The U.S. Federal Communications Commission (FCC) fined his radio show for indecency and
obscenity violations, and he's famous for his interviews of prosti-
tutes, lesbians, and adult-movie stars—often in various stages of
undress. He's not the first entertainer to realize that sex and obscenity sells, but he's perhaps the greatest master of it on the air-
waves. His radio show had about 12 million daily listeners during
2005, and his television show had an average of 1 million viewers
each weekday. The radio and television networks that air his
shows make millions each year from advertisers seeking to reach

his viewers, many of whom, not surprisingly, are men between the ages of eighteen and thirty-four.[1]

Come 2006, though, you couldn't hear Stern on traditional radio anymore. The FCC didn't shut him down, nor did his advertisers bolt from his bad-boy image. He became central to what we have called a "marquee" strategy for Sirius Satellite Radio—the number-two satellite radio company in the United States. Sirius paid him more than $500 million, plus additional payments based on performance, to air his radio show exclusively for five years. Americans can hear Stern's radio show only if they subscribe to Sirius.

Stern could justify his hefty paychecks by bringing in many listeners who could help fuel a catalytic reaction. His show should help Sirius sell more subscriptions, and this should help it attract more advertisers for all its channels that have advertisements. It is still too early to tell whether this huge bet on a marquee strategy will pay off. But it has fueled growth: between the time of the announced deal with Stern and the time his radio show first aired (October 2004 to January 2006), Sirius got 2.6 million additional subscribers—an astounding 400 percent increase over fifteen months.[2]

Sirius and its bigger rival, XM Satellite Radio, have shown patience in building up this new method for delivering music, sports, and entertainment to radio. They started work on their ventures in the early 1990s. XM launched its nationwide satellite radio service in November 2001, and Sirius in July 2002. Although still youngsters with lots of opportunities for success and failure before them, and stock prices that have had a roller-coaster ride, they threaten to take a substantial audience share from U.S. terrestrial radio broadcasters.

Sirius and XM recognized the importance of experimentation in discovering how to ignite a catalytic reaction and of adopting an evolutionary—rather than a big bang—strategy for growth. Experimenting and evolving in this way is the final element of the catalyst framework, as shown in figure 8-1.

In this chapter, we focus on several key tasks a catalyst entrepreneur ought to pursue to ensure successful growth:

1. **Know when to be first—and when to follow.** Don't overlook the advantages of starting slow and building gradually. It is easier to adjust pricing, design, and other

FIGURE 8-1

The catalyst framework: experiment and evolve

Identify the platform community	Establish a pricing structure	Design the catalyst for success	Focus on profitability	Compete strategically with other catalysts	**Experiment and evolve**
• Identify distinct groups that need each other	• Set separate prices for access and usage	• Attract multiple customer groups that need each other	• Study industry history	• Understand the dynamics of catalyst competition	• Know when to be first—and when to follow
• Determine why and how much they need each other	• Set prices to balance demand from two sides	• Promote interactions	• Use forecasts to enhance profitability	• Look for competition from different business models	• Control growth
• Evaluate who else is serving the community	• Price to grow slowly—at first	• Minimize transaction costs	• Anticipate competitor actions		• Protect your back
• Compare a multisided business model with a single-sided one	• Pay customers to belong—sometimes	• Design for evolution	• Align interests internally and externally	• Leverage to attack	• Plan for what's next
	• Price for long-term profits			• Consider cooperation	• Look out for the cops
Find out who needs whom—and why	**Shape participation and maximize profits**	**Draw customers and facilitate interactions**	**Visualize path toward long-term profit**	**Challenge existing catalysts and react to new catalyst threats**	**Pursue evolutionary strategy for growth**

strategies before you have made significant, irreversible investments. At the same time, examine the possible advantages of being a market pioneer.

2. **Control growth.** Have a strategy for growing the business on your terms and in your time frame. Often that means adopting a business model that allows you to expand the platform—geographically, for example—while maintaining control over pricing, design, and other key strategies for harnessing the power of the catalytic reaction.

3. **Protect your back.** Having seen your success, other entrepreneurs will build on what you have learned. Being first doesn't guarantee success. Being paranoid helps.

4. **Plan for what's next.** Have a plan for when your platform reaches saturation, and consider other catalyst products to build from this platform.

5. **Watch out for the cops.** As a catalyst, you will find that courts and regulators probably won't understand what you do, and if you get big, they will be suspicious. Help them understand how your business model makes all your customer groups better off before the cops come knocking at your door.

Task 1: Know When to Be First— and When to Follow

XM radio beat Sirius to market by almost a year. It has a significant lead as of 2006. Will it maintain it? XM's investors shouldn't take comfort in the history of catalysts.

Being first and fast doesn't guarantee a catalyst's success. Google was so late to the search engine party that it tried to sell its technology to the established players. Told by one to "go pound sand," Google quickly overtook these rivals. Some readers might remember that the Apple Newton was the first personal digital assistant. The Newton fizzled, and the Palm Pilot ignited the catalyst reaction for PDAs a few years after Apple's first move. And Sirius's marquee strategy helped narrow the gap with XM. Sirius had a fifth as many subscribers as XM at the time of the Stern announcement and three-fifths as many a month after Stern's showed aired.

Nevertheless, being the first catalyst to market can create some significant advantages.

Business Wire, to take one example, started a catalyst reaction between companies that wanted to distribute press releases and other material to newspapers and wire services. Lorry Lokey started this company in October 1961 in San Francisco to distribute press releases to the media. From these small beginnings, it has grown into a comprehensive platform that enables companies to dispense information to more than sixty leading news agencies throughout the world and allows news organizations throughout the world to obtain access to this information. With only one serious rival, Lokey's company has dominated the business he created almost half a century ago. (Berkshire Hathaway bought the privately owned Business Wire in early 2006.)

What we see in the evolution of successful catalysts confirms the wisdom in two seemingly contradictory old sayings: "The early bird gets the worm" and "Haste makes waste."

The advantages of being the first catalyst in a market can be substantial. Catalytic reactions are fueled by positive feedbacks between the different customer groups. Whoever starts these feedbacks first and revs them up the fastest will make life hard for its late-coming rivals. Business Wire used positive feedbacks to get most content outlets to distribute its material. That makes it a challenge for others to get into this business.

Scale economies (as shown in figure 8-2) and steep learning curves can also advantage first movers. These can be especially important for catalysts, such as satellite radio, that depend upon manufacturers to make components, and for catalysts, such as those based on software platforms and physical exchanges, that incur large fixed costs that can be averaged down across a larger base of customers. By getting in first and growing quickly, a catalyst can secure lower costs of production that give it an advantage

FIGURE 8-2

Scale economies

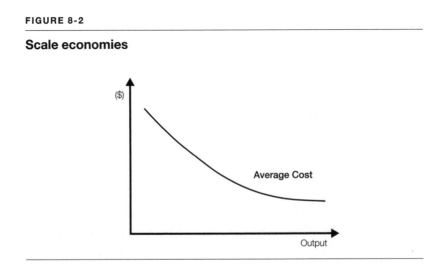

over later and smaller entrants. Digital Research's CP/M operating system was one of the first entrants into software platforms in the late 1970s. It and other early entrants failed in part because they didn't grow quickly: they priced their software too high to take advantage of potential scale economies and positive feedbacks.

The pioneering catalyst can also establish a business model that plays to its strengths and may make it more difficult for copycat catalysts to compete. If the first mover decides to encourage one side to join the reaction by offering a low price, or even offering inducements, the second and later entrants will find it hard to get in without offering the same deal. That means the first mover can decide on which side to subsidize in part according to whether it has a special advantage in serving that side that its rivals won't have. In industries where there are scarce assets—one can argue whether this description fits Howard Stern—pioneering firms may be able to capture them on advantageous terms. And first movers may be able to create "switching costs" of various sorts that make their customers reluctant to leave when new alternatives appear in the market.

Thus the "network effects" gurus and the investment banking analysts who echoed them were right that being first and fast could help businesses secure dominant positions. They did not, however, recognize that there are many elements of a successful catalyst strategy beyond generating positive feedback and exploiting scale economies. Nor were they mindful of how important experimentation and learning are to a young catalyst trying to seek the proper balance for harnessing the power of the catalytic reaction.

That is why we have to consider another well-worn saying: "Haste makes waste." It is interesting that many successful catalysts have not been pioneers in their markets, but rather the fast followers of others who failed to get their businesses right. American Express, Google, Sony, Palm, and the online version of the *Wall Street Journal* are all examples of companies that were second—or later—but that learned valuable lessons from those that went before.

Haste often leads to several problems in catalyst businesses. Perhaps the most embarrassing one is spending a fortune on establishing a platform for a catalyst reaction and having one or more critical groups not show up for the opening party. That's what happened to Zethus, one of many Internet start-ups that saw riches in challenging traditional real estate brokers. Backed by Goldman Sachs, it tried to create an online exchange for the fragmented commercial real estate industry. The idea was that brokers, such as commercial real estate giant Cushman and Wakefield, would post a proposal for space, identifying the type of tenant, the space requirements, and the lease duration. Property owners would then submit bids over the next twenty-four hours. Nice idea, but hardly anyone came to the party. Most commercial brokers didn't see what they were going to get out of this system, and without the brokers, the commercial landlords didn't sign on either. Zethus hadn't carefully investigated whether any significant part of its proposed community saw value in its exchange. Commercial real estate is based on intimate knowledge of properties, landlords, and tenants and on personal relationships. Online bidding didn't add value to this. So Zethus's business model, which was based on taking a percentage of the transaction, didn't work because few wanted to close deals using its service. Zethus never launched a product, and, despite its blue-chip backing, the company filed for bankruptcy in March 2001. It died quickly because it hadn't learned what a major part of its community really wanted. It might have learned and adjusted its business strategy if it had shown more patience.

Speed also makes it harder to fix pricing problems. Consider a catalyst that charges too low a price to one side and too high a price to another side and tries to expand quickly. Many members of the low-priced community sign up, only to learn that the catalyst can't deliver much value because few members of the high-priced community have shown up. Moreover, the low-priced community has been conditioned to expect a low price. The catalyst may have difficulty trying to get them to pay the higher price it needs to be viable.

For example, *Slate*, the online opinion magazine, started life in 1996 as a free Web site with such brand-name advertisers as AT&T, Ford Motor Company, and Fidelity Investments. In the following three years, *Slate* flip-flopped between charging subscription fees and making content available for free. Not surprisingly, Slate's site traffic rose and fell substantially, as did its advertising volume. The competition—and benefactor of the abused advertising and user community—was *Salon* magazine. *Salon* started out free and stayed that way, making it difficult, if not impossible, for

Slate with its sometimes free, sometimes not model to attract visitors or advertisers. Once *Slate*'s management realized that it was "spending 90% of the time on content that hardly anyone saw . . . with visitor traffic too sparse to attract many advertisers," it became free for good.[3]

We draw several lessons from the trade-off between being first and fast on the one hand and being a methodical follower on the other hand:

THE LESSONS

Catalysts should err on the side of being first and fast when positive feedback effects and scale economies are so important that it is clear that one catalyst will come to dominate the category. The first one in with the right business model will capture the catalyst category.

Catalysts should err on the side of being a methodical follower when it is clear that through product differentiation or because positive feedbacks and scale economies are weak, several firms can serve the catalyst community. Learn from the mistakes of the rash early entrants.

Catalysts should err on the side of being slow and methodical when it is unclear what the right community, pricing, and design strategies are for igniting and maintaining a profitable catalyst reaction. It is better to stay small and get things right before expanding.

Task 2: Grow with Control

Catalysts, like all businesses, want to grow. But simply trying to grow as quickly as possible isn't always a practical solution for companies that need to maintain the delicate balance among the multiple sides of its community. A task of a catalyst is to determine what strategy it wants to pursue to drive and control its growth. Here we look at three options: scalable growth, cooperative growth, and replication.

Satellite radio has grown more rapidly than many other technologies for delivering entertainment to the American public, as shown in figure 8-3.

Between 2001 and 2005, Sirius and XM acquired 9 million subscribers between them. After we adjust for the smaller size of the population, it took six years for commercial terrestrial radio, twenty-four years for cable television, and eight years for mobile telephones to attain the same levels of penetration. Yet both satellite radio pioneers have worked methodically at building communities that will help fuel sustained profitable growth.

To understand their growth strategies, it helps to consider the mature business these rivals of traditional radio hope to achieve. They'll derive profits from subscribers who will pay annual fees and from advertisers that will pay to reach these subscribers. They'll probably depend on third parties to build radios for use in homes and automobiles. If they become popular enough, they'll be

FIGURE 8-3

Adoption rates of various entertainment and communications media

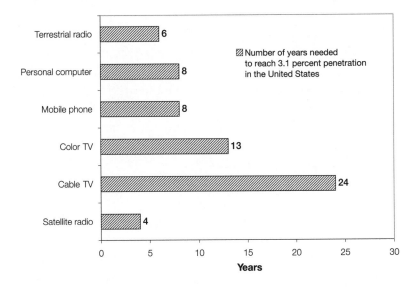

Source: Internal Market Platform Dynamics research

able to depend on automobile makers to include satellite radios in most models as an option or perhaps even as standard equipment. Instead of trying to make money by licensing their technology to manufacturers, they are more likely to find that it is better to have zero license fees, to keep satellite radios as cheap as possible. If they become stable, mature businesses, Sirius and XM probably won't need to pay as much for other premier content as Sirius did for Howard Stern. Marquee content is more important to ignite a new reaction than to sustain a healthy, mature one. To reach this vision, XM and Sirius would need to grow relatively slowly as the catalyst community around satellite radio grows and becomes more devoted.

They can't get from here to there with one big splash. As youngsters, Sirius and XM couldn't count on these groups to help sustain a catalyst reaction. Radio manufacturers didn't have much interest in making satellite radios for consumers. Because few consumers had subscribed, it didn't make much business sense for them to produce at mass-market scales that would have justified reasonable prices. So Sirius and XM had to contract with manufacturers to produce the necessary hardware for their services and, as they grew, to make more sophisticated radios. By early 2006, a wide variety of satellite radio products were available to consumers. Likewise, they couldn't count on automakers to design dashboards that provided the convenient and attractive consumer interface that was to be a key differentiator from terrestrial radio. So they had to help the automakers with design gratis, even though their products helped sell more automobiles. By the end of 2005, more than 38.3 percent of new cars available for sale in the United States had satellite radio listed as an option, and more than 5.2 million drivers had in-dash Sirius or XM receivers in their cars.[4]

Sirius and XM have adopted a *scalable* growth strategy. They started with a modest group of subscribers and advertisers. Mainly through encouraging positive feedback effects, they hope to attain an increasing number of subscribers and advertisers over time. They also hope to find an increasing number of manufacturers interested in helping to sustain their ecosystem and expect to cede most of the operational control over the hardware side of their business as that happens. As of the summer of 2006, both satellite radio companies are facing challenges to continuing their growth and achieving profitability. That should not be taken as a criticism of their catalyst business model nor of their pursuit of scalable growth. It may simply be a tough market.

MasterCard and Visa built global card systems through a *cooperative strategy*. By the mid-1960s, many American banks had tried to start card programs, with little success. Several realized that they could get enough geographic reach and enough capital to compete with American Express and Diners Club only if they banded together. They agreed that any merchant they signed up would accept a card issued by any member of the cooperative, and that any cardholder they signed up could use their card at a merchant serviced by any member of the cooperative. MasterCard was the first to do this on a national basis in 1966. Visa copied this highly successful model five years later. Both card systems grew by letting more banks into their associations in the United States. They then let either banks or associations of banks overseas into their cooperatives. As of 2005, MasterCard and Visa each had more than twenty thousand bank members around the world.[5]

Like many cooperatives, MasterCard and Visa have struggled with the tension between members that compete with each other on some dimensions but cooperate for their greater good on other dimensions. They are akin in some ways to political institutions where checks and balances are used to prevent tyrannies of the majority or the minority. And they implement many rules that force members to adhere to standards and practices that advance the brand and that prevent some members from behaving opportunistically or free-riding on the efforts of the cooperative.

Other catalysts have followed a *replication strategy*. They just multiply copies of themselves for different communities. With a handful of employees, craigslist has created replicas of its classified advertising, real estate listings, entertainment guides, and other online services for more than three hundred cities around the world as of August 2006. 8minuteDating has followed a similar approach. It started in Boston in 2001 and made its frenetic dating service available in more than eighty cities in the United States by November 2006.[6]

Looking across successful catalysts that have grown their businesses, we see two lessons:

THE LESSONS

Pick the right strategy for growth. Catalysts should decide whether the nature of their business lends itself to adopting a scalable, cooperative, or replicable platform.

Maintain control over community relations, design, and pricing as you grow. That's easy with a scalable platform because it is typically subject to centralized control. That's harder for cooperative and replicable platforms, which necessarily require some ceding of control to others.

Task 3: Protect Your Back

As we saw in the last chapter, competition—often in the form of imitation—is always a threat to a catalyst. But that does not mean that steps can't be taken by pioneer catalysts to make life difficult for potential challengers.

Alibaba was not the first to see opportunities from linking China's small businesses into global supply chains. But with more than 9 million registered users, it is the biggest to have done this online. Like many other Internet businesses, Alibaba built its user base by providing services for free. But it succeeded where others haven't, by identifying value-added services that users are willing for pay for.

Seeing the opportunity to create not only a large but trusted online marketplace, Alibaba launched TrustPass in 2002. This program uses third-party credit agencies to authenticate and verify the identity and other information about users (mostly small suppliers in China). TrustPass is an extension of Alibaba's transaction history and feedback systems that build the online credibility of buyers and sellers over time, literally transaction by transaction. These sorts of historical feedback systems cannot be easily copied by new competitors and can create a high entry barrier for new entrants.

Even though the authentication service costs nearly $300 per user, users have flocked to sign up.

Many catalysts use intellectual property rights to protect themselves, as do many other companies in our high-technology age. These were essential to many two-sided companies we've examined—from NTT DoCoMo's i-mode system, to Microsoft Windows, to Sony's PlayStation. Even an older industry such as payment cards is also full of legal protections that make it very hard for a new imitator to enter the market. Besides their trademarked global brands, American Express, MasterCard, and Visa together hold more than 150 patents that cover everything from Visa's "Self-paying smart utility meter" to MasterCard's "Combined card binder and card."

The other most reliable source of protection for a catalyst comes from simply maintaining the strength of the community through the techniques we have seen in earlier chapters. Sirius Satellite Radio has exclusive contracts with marquee content such as Howard Stern that other competitors cannot imitate. Other catalysts, such as eBay, have built into their businesses features such as the feedback system that have become highly valued to the community, even if others could create similar tools. The ability to maintain the trust and ease of use of a service—especially online—can be an important barrier to lesser-known market entrants.

One final strategy, used by some catalysts as well as many other businesses, is to invest in differentiation—either by offering goods or services that competitors can't readily match or by investing in building a reputation that will provide long-term profits. When the NASDAQ stock market began trading in 1971, it was the world's first electronic stock market. Most consumers don't know that, however. They are more likely to have seen ads, particularly during the dot-com boom, stressing how many technology companies are listed on NASDAQ and touting it as "the stock market for the next hundred years." NASDAQ was also the first stock market to advertise to the general public, and it has aggressively pursued a differentiation strategy to maintain and strengthen its market position against its leading downtown competitor, the New York Stock Exchange (NYSE).

Having the advantage of being early is great. Catalysts that want to keep that lead should heed several lessons that all successful firms have learned:

THE LESSONS

Secure your intellectual property rights. Many catalysts have to make investments in new technology to establish their platforms and to get members to interact. Catalysts should make sure they have availed themselves of patents, copyrights, and trademarks to protect their intellectual property and to rely on trade secret protection where they can't.

Secure your community relationships. Catalysts create value by earning the allegiance of several groups. Providing good value is perhaps the most important way any business can make sure its customers stay loyal. But catalysts can also rely on exclusive contracts—that's what Sirius radio has with Howard Stern and XM with Major League Baseball. They can also try to make sure that customers are getting something of value they can't get elsewhere. EBay's feedback system provides sellers with an asset—their reported reputation—that they wouldn't be able to get on a new competitor.

Secure differentiators. This is particularly important when positive feedback and scale can't protect your investments or you are challenging a bigger catalyst. You must find a way to provide value to some segment of the catalyst community that others will have trouble matching.

Task 4: Plan for What's Next

Nippon Telephone and Telegraph (NTT) built DoCoMo, which we discussed in the last chapter, into the leading mobile telephone operator in Japan. By 1996, 16 percent of Japanese residents had a mobile phone, 40 percent of which were from DoCoMo.[7] And penetration was increasing explosively. Soon just about everyone would have a phone. The plateau of the famous S curve of product cycles was in sight. Where would growth come after that?

DoCoMo recognized that it needed to find another S curve to jump on. Getting people to call each other more was one way to do that. More traffic, more revenue. But people can spend only so much time talking on the phone.

As we discussed in chapter 3, DoCoMo ignited a second catalytic reaction by developing a phone-based Web portal called i-mode. It created a software platform based on Internet standards. That made it easy for content providers to make their content available for the new portal. It also built a community of content providers that created specific sites that would make the i-mode service appealing. These content providers were able to use DoCoMo's convenient billing system and kept more than 90 percent of the revenues they got from i-mode users. Mobile users flocked to the content, which included ringtones, contact organizers, horoscopes, mobile banking, news, games, and sports. Figure 8-4 shows DoCoMo's voice and data revenue, from

FIGURE 8-4

The impact of i-mode on DoCoMo cellular service revenue

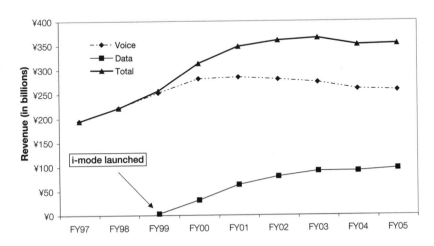

Sources: NTT DoCoMo Annual Report 2001; "NTT DoCoMo—IR—Annual/Quarterly Results," NTT Do-CoMo website, http://www.nttdocomo.co.jp/english/corporate/investor_relations/business/fiscal_e.html; Morgan Stanley Equity Research, investment reports on NTT DoCoMo, various issues

which one can see that i-mode was responsible for all of DoCoMo's growth in recent years.

What we have seen in the DoCoMo experience and elsewhere is that there are several lessons for catalysts that want to understand how to evolve and experiment to sustain growth:

THE LESSONS

Examine whether your catalyst business will reach a plateau where further growth is not possible under your current business model. Catalysts grow by getting more members of customer groups on their platforms and getting these customers to interact more with each other. Catalysts should forecast when these sources of growth will weaken. DoCoMo realized in the mid-1990s that they couldn't count on more customers or more customer interactions, with their business model at the time, to fuel future growth in Japanese mobile phone revenues. The fifty-year-old credit card industry in the United States reached its plateau in the early 2000s. Almost everyone who wants a credit card now has several, and growth in borrowing on cards has slowed to a crawl. As of 2006, credit card issuers don't appear to have a plan for moving to another S curve, and the industry is becoming a low-margin, scale-driven, commodity business. Terrestrial radio passively watched its growth flatten and left itself vulnerable to the new satellite catalysts.

Examine new features or line extensions that could add fuel to the catalytic reaction (see the box "Evolution of the Octopus Card "). Catalysts based on software platforms have incorporated this approach as part of their business models. They add new features every few years to attract more developers and users. The number of lines of code in software platforms doubles about every two years as a result of adding more services for members of the several groups supported by the code.

Plan for the next S curve. Instead of seeking incremental growth from new features and line extensions, consider ways of leveraging your catalyst community to start a whole new catalytic reaction. Obviously, that is the toughest challenge,

Evolution of the Octopus Card

Originally launched as a convenient fare collection system for Hong Kong's mass transit system, the Octopus card has expanded to become a widely used electronic cash product that enjoys a 95 percent penetration of Hong Kong residents between the ages of sixteen and sixty-five. With over 14 million cards in circulation, what began as a transit card is now accepted at more than 370 merchants and transport operators and operates as an access card and timekeeping device at schools, public buildings, and recreational facilities.[8] Figure 8-5 tracks its evolution.

The Octopus card is also refillable; more than twenty-two banks offer convenient refillable services for up to $500 Hong Kong dollars (about 64 US dollars).[9] This multipurpose card has an attractive value proposition for merchants and cardholders: it's fast, efficient, and secure. It's even recently given birth to a whole line of branded Octopus items, key fobs, watches, and phones—each of which can be used to pay with a wave—and a rewards program that offers cash-back rewards for cardholders at participating retailers.

FIGURE 8-5

The evolution of a catalyst: the Octopus card

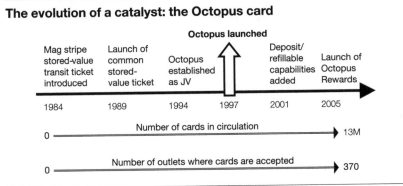

and few catalysts succeed in doing it. But consider American Express, which has ridden at least three S curves in its 150-year history. It started as a mail service that had a fleet of stagecoaches and pony express riders to deliver mail. At the end of the nineteenth century, it created the traveler's check. It got merchants to accept this form of payment and consumers to use it. After a bit more than half a century, it started a charge card business. And as growth in the charge card business slowed, it got a credit card business off the ground that, after a rocky start, has become quite successful. (Even so, the credit card industry seems ripe for evolution; for more, see the box "Credit Card's Midlife Crisis.")

Credit Card's Midlife Crisis

Credit cards have lost a lot of their pizzazz. Early on, this innovative product allowed consumers to do something they once only dreamed of: make purchases today and pay for them tomorrow. For issuers and consumers both, this was a significant innovation. Issuers once counted on consumers to rack up borrowing on their cards and collected a tidy profit on financing these receivables. And consumers did just that—U.S. consumers owed more than $700 billion to credit card issuers in 2004, about eight times more (in constant dollars) than twenty years earlier.[10]

But the meteoric growth in borrowing came to a grinding halt a few years ago. The historical drivers of increased borrowing have run their course, and issuers seem to have been caught unprepared. Instead of creating product innovations and growing the market, the credit card business seems to have stagnated. Stealing share is now the name of the game. Banks flood consumers' mailboxes with solicitations in an attempt to lure customers from competitors, but the returns on direct mail have dropped sharply. Overall, borrowing isn't growing much, so neither are the finance fees that go with it. Credit card issuers have been able to count on interchange fee revenues (paid by mer-

Task 5: Look Out for the Cops

Until the beginning of this century, no one understood that industries as diverse as auction houses, video games, traveler's checks, magazines, real estate, stock markets, and singles bars were catalysts that created value by getting different communities of customers together. When people tried to understand how these industries operated, they considered them in isolation. And looked at that way, they each engaged in practices that looked quite strange to quite knowledgeable people who were well versed in how traditional businesses operated.

---

chants' banks as a percentage of the amount charged) to keep their cards in the black. Although interchange fees have increased in recent years, those increases can't and thus won't continue forever. The class action lawsuits that have been filed recently should make banks worry that their interchange fee income might, instead, start to decline.

Given the increased competition and slowed borrowing, banks have tried to create new sources of revenue. Instead of enhancing their products, they have added or modified fees and other card features, such as the length of the grace period and the fee for late payment. Some of these changes aren't all that transparent to cardholders. The result is irritated consumers, a few lawsuits, and an increased level of government scrutiny.

The credit card industry has reached middle age and it appears time to make plans for the next stage of its life. Ironically, the power of innovation that fueled the industry in its youth has all but dissipated. In order to avoid the fate of refrigerators, toasters, and other products that stagnated late in their life cycles, credit card issuers now must examine whether there are new ways to leverage their card assets into other kinds of business while seeking ways to build on the value proposition that built the business—an easy-to-use, safe way to pay and borrow.

Unfortunately, human nature makes us distrust what is different and what we don't understand. And as a result, catalysts have had more than their fair share of run-ins with government authorities, not to mention the media, that tend to see chicanery in business practices that don't fit traditional molds. Microsoft's brush with antitrust authorities in the United States is a good example.

The government suggested that there was something wrong with Microsoft's spending millions to persuade developers to write thousands of applications for the Windows operating system even though it received no revenue from them. The government contended that having succeeded at this task gave Microsoft an unfair advantage over other operating system vendors. What it didn't recognize was that operating systems are catalysts that serve communities of developers, users, hardware makers, and possibly other groups as well. All operating systems compete by encouraging application developers and others to make complementary products that help consumers. Microsoft may have crossed the line in other actions that it took—courts found some of its conduct monopolistic—but encouraging developers to write applications was and remains an essential part of the catalytic reaction that created value for the many communities this operating system served.

Complex businesses like catalysts often make for complex questions of business ethics. Payola is one example. In the United States, music publishers sometimes pay radio stations to play particular songs. The discovery and public exposure of this practice back in the 1960s led to a law declaring such "payola" a criminal offense. Yet in economic terms, one could argue that pay for play was just another form of advertising for the radio stations—advertising of songs. In the early days of radio, music publishers provided music for free in the hopes that it would encourage consumers to buy records. As radio got more popular, music publishers believed they had a right to collect royalties on their music, and they were able to use the copyright laws to force radio stations to pay for this content. However, the music publishers still had incentives sometimes to discount those royalties—and possibly pay the stations outright—so that the stations would play content that would drive sales of records.

This is not to deny that payola raises an ethical issue—the same one that the advertising-supported search engine catalysts of the early twenty-first century have grappled with, as advertising-supported newspapers have done for decades. Should there be a strict separation between content and advertising? Google decided that advertising revenue shouldn't influence its search results: you can't pay to get higher placement in a search, although you can pay to be a clearly labeled sponsored link at the top of the page or have a clearly labeled advertisement on the right-hand side of page. Many newspapers similarly treat the editorial and advertising sides of their business as "church and state."

Our study of catalysts suggests that these separations are based on good business reasons that may also be ethically sound. Catalysts are constantly balancing the value they provide each of the communities they serve. Letting advertisers affect search results, advertising, or music selection helps advertisers but may degrade the value of the content for users. Newspapers and search engines have products in which credibility is important to users. We suspect the influence of payola on radio station listeners was much less severe and that the stations decided that the added advertising revenue was worth biasing the playing of songs somewhat.

Government authorities are often quite suspicious when they see catalysts impose rules or restrictions that limit what customers can do. Surcharging for payment cards is a good example. Since the early days of the industry, payment card systems have prohibited merchants from assessing card customers an extra fee for using their cards instead of cash or checks. That no-surcharge rule makes cards less desirable to merchants but more desirable to cardholders. Card systems found that was the right balance. Both merchants and cardholders could factor that feature into their decisions of whether to take and to use cards. Regulators in a few countries, such as Australia and the United Kingdom, have forced card systems to allow merchants to add on surcharges. Most merchants don't do this, but often those that do tack on quite large surcharges—more than the price they pay for taking the card—to exploit customers who don't have any other way to pay.

Most governments don't start paying attention to businesses until they get big and powerful, and that tends to be true for catalysts. So if you are just starting out and remain small, you don't need to worry much about the cops coming after you because you seem different. But as you grow, it helps to be prepared by taking notice of several lessons:

THE LESSONS

Help the media, legislators, regulators, and other influential people understand how your business operates.

Show these influential people that you aren't that different—that you follow strategies common in your industry and employed by catalysts in many other industries as well.

Recognize that certain practices—such as pricing below cost, entering into exclusive deals, letting advertising affect content decisions, and imposing restrictions on your customers—are likely to draw scrutiny.

Rely on transparency and honesty. If you are a broker, make sure that customers know who is paying for your services and which party you represent. If you are in advertising-supported media, make sure that consumers know how advertising is affecting content decisions.

Experiment, Evolve, and the Catalyst Framework

Catalysts are naturally growth businesses. Positive feedbacks between communities provide the fuel for that growth. Catalysts are also naturally unstable businesses. They succeed only when they keep their balance. Like bicyclists, catalysts can move forward while staying upright only by constantly adjusting their motion. They must constantly experiment to keep the catalytic reaction going. And they must evolve in the face of almost certain threats from competing single- and multisided businesses. How to do this is summarized in table 8-1.

TiVo exemplifies the challenges that catalysts face. It pioneered a digital video recorder (DVR) whose software recorded television shows and stripped out the commercials. Many television aficionados took to it like bees to honey. The sophisticated software made it

TABLE 8-1

Experiment, evolve, and the catalyst framework

Tasks	Lessons
Know when to be first, when to follow.	• Be first and fast when positive feedback effects and scale economies are critical. • Be a follower when positive feedback is weak and several firms can serve the community.
Control growth.	• Pick the right strategy for growth. • Adopt a scalable, cooperative, or replicable platform. • Maintain control over community relations, design, and pricing as you grow.
Protect your back.	• Secure intellectual property rights. • Secure community relationships. • Secure differentiators.
Plan for what's next.	• Examine whether your catalyst business will reach a plateau. • Examine new features or line extensions. • Plan for the next S curve.
Watch out for the cops.	• Make sure authorities understand your business. • Show authorities how your practices are common in the catalyst industry. • Expect scrutiny of normal catalyst business practices. • Rely on transparency and honesty.

far more convenient to program than traditional video recorders, and dodging the commercials was like a dream come true. DIRECTV— a U.S. satellite television provider—and several cable companies decided that this was an attractive product for their customers. TiVo ended up distributing its boxes directly to consumers and indirectly through its allies.

TiVo realized early on that it had a platform that not only could eliminate distracting television advertisements but could provide alternative advertisements that would be of more value to both viewers and advertisers. As it developed its base of users, TiVo started inserting advertisements that viewers could select if they were interested. TiVo could offer Jaguar the opportunity to make a five-minute video on its new Jaguar XK convertible available to consumers as an option. Consumers can click on a "branded tag" if they want to see the video. Relatively few will do so, but they will begin with well-above-average interest, and they will see much more than a standard thirty-second spot. Long-form video clips from advertisers are also available in the "showcase" folder in TiVo's menu, where users are also able to watch previews of movies or TV programs. Thus TiVo saw its future as a two-sided business that would earn revenues from both advertisers and viewers.

While the company has dedicated—perhaps even fanatic—followers, it has yet to earn a profit. It has more than 4.4 million subscribers, but that's less than 4 percent of American households.[11] It has had trouble expanding beyond dedicated couch potatoes. Meanwhile, it is facing competition from several directions. Cable- and satellite-television providers are introducing their own DVRs, competing with TiVo at lower prices. For example, TiVo's biggest ally, DIRECTV, which had delivered roughly 64 percent of TiVo's subscribers, started offering its own DVR in addition to TiVo's. And big consumer electronics manufacturers, such as Scientific Atlanta and Motorola, are selling their own DVRs through the cable companies that buy their other equipment. They have been resistant to ceding this territory to TiVo. At the same time, many players are developing video-on-demand and Internet television based on software technology that isn't tied to the box that TiVo has pushed. In 2005 Comcast began providing free access to video-on-demand content, and Verizon began testing Internet-based TV services (which included on-demand services) over its fiber-optic network.

TiVo is at a cusp where its catalytic reaction will either take off or fizzle. It is actively working on expanding its software technology so that people can control their records with their mobile phones. And it is well positioned to attract advertisers that are looking for television viewers who want to watch their advertisements and are therefore likely to buy, just as Google has done for newspapers' advertisements. Whether it can attract a critical mass of advertisers and viewers, quickly enough, in the face of rivals at its back and by its side, remains to be seen.

9

Cracking the Catalyst Code

I am hell-bent for the South Pole—
God willing and crevasses permitting.

—SIR EDMUND HILLARY

IT WOULD BE A MISTAKE TO ASSUME THAT CATALYSTS ARE merely a faddish business model, fueled by technology and the Internet. As we have tried to show in this book, catalysts have existed for millennia, even as we witness a remarkable boom in catalyst business in our own day. Today our understanding of how catalysts work and how they thrive is better than ever. The recent work of economists has allowed us to view the catalyst not simply as an interesting business arrangement but as a very carefully constructed set of relationships that become an engine for economic growth and profitability. We can apply that understanding not only to the modern electronic and virtual business sites but also to long-established companies whose success has never been fully explained.

Indeed, some of the most instructive catalysts are centuries old. They have shown incredible durability not simply because they were well managed, nor because they were merely lucky to emerge when they did. Many businesses endure because they have cracked the catalyst code.

Durable Catalysts

In 1744, Samuel Baker auctioned off an estate library of 457 books. The "Several Hundred Scarce and Valuable Books in all Branches of Polite Literature" fetched £826 ($210,048 in today's dollars), from which Mr. Baker no doubt received a healthy commission. After his death in 1778, a nephew, John Sotheby, inherited part ownership in his firm. The Sotheby clan played a critical role in building the firm into one of the premier auctioneers of books and manuscripts over the next eighty years.

As with many catalysts, intricate relationships lie behind the simple façade of the auction. Developing a community of buyers and sellers in England, Europe, and the new United States was critical. Sotheby and his partners worked with dealers who bought rare books but didn't have ready access to enough buyers. And since displaying rare books and illuminated manuscripts was part of the lifestyle of the superrich in the nineteenth century, they courted the many men who earned fortunes during the industrial revolution. Reputation was important as well. Sotheby's was known for its acumen in assessing the value and authenticity of the rare books, manuscripts, prints, and other material in which it specialized.

Sotheby's wasn't the leading auction house in the mid-nineteenth century, nor would it be for well over another hundred years—it was far behind the more fashionable house founded by and named for James Christie, whose first auction consisted of several bales of hay, lots of Madeira, and some "Flavour'd Claret." Christie was a friend of many of the leading artists of his day, and his auction house soon specialized in fine art. Indeed, for many years, the two firms had a nice cooperative arrangement. Christie's would send rare books over to Sotheby's, and Sotheby's would ship fine art over to Christie's.

That arrangement ended early in the twentieth century, when Sotheby's got new owners and management. It took on Christie's in the art market, and a great catalyst clash emerged between the two firms. In recent years, the two auction houses have been neck and neck in terms of sales. In 2004, Sotheby's had the highest sales, but Christie's acquired the top spot in 2005. It had sales of £1.8 billion, while Sotheby's was just below with £1.6 billion. In 2005, the average price of each lot sold by Sotheby's was about $37,500—a value much greater than Christie's average of $20,100.[1] (Sadly, in the 1990s, leaders of the two firms colluded on the prices they were charging. They were subject to criminal charges in the United States, which is why Alfred Taubman, who had invested in Sotheby's in 1983, spent time behind bars. Both firms have since recovered.)

Today, of course, both Sotheby's and Christie's find themselves challenged by a new catalyst business that has none of their history or pedigree: eBay. The history here reminds us that in the catalyst world (as in the single-sided world), being either the first mover or a fast follower is not a guarantor of success. As we see in table 9-1, there is a rich history among catalyst businesses of an impressive innovator that first solves the chicken-and-egg problem central to every catalyst only to be rapidly displaced by a follower that does it better. Moreover, as we saw with payment cards, video games, and television networks, new competitors can supplant both the innovator and the fast follower. Sony did it to Atari and Nintendo in the video game market—just as Xbox is now trying to oust Sony as the market leader.

In 1776, the *Pennsylvania Evening Post* was the first newspaper to report that the United States was preparing to declare its independence from Britain, bringing together readers and advertisers to its pages. Despite this historic scoop—and the powerful catalyst model the paper had created—a rival emerged in the form of the *Pennsylvania Packet and Daily Advertiser,* which went on to become the first truly successful daily newspaper in the country. Today neither paper exists. The leading print newspaper catalyst is *USA Today,* which is not aimed at or based in any specific local community, departing from the formula used by most popular

TABLE 9-1

Famous followers

Category	The first	The fast follower	2006 market leader[a]
Payment cards	Diners Club	National Credit Card	Visa
Video games	Atari	Nintendo	Sony
PC operating systems	CP/M	IBM DOS	Microsoft Windows
TV network	NBC (the first network to introduce regular television in the United States in 1939)	CBS (also in 1939)	CBS
Daily newspaper	*Pennsylvania Evening Post*	*Pennsylvania Packet and Daily Advertiser*	*USA Today*
Boston downtown shopping area	Downtown Crossing in Boston	Newbury Street, Boston	Copley Plaza, Boston
Auction houses	Sotheby's	Christie's	eBay

Sources: "National Broadcasting Company," The Museum of Broadcast Communications Web site, http://www.museum.tv/archives/etv/N/htmlN/nationalbroa/nationalbroa.htm; Daya Kishan Thussu, "International Communication: Continuity and Change," *Business & Economics,* 2001; "The Nation's First Daily Newspaper Began Publication," America's Story from America's Library Web site, http://www.americas story.com/cgi-bin/page.cgi/jb/revolut/newspap_2; and *Editor & Publisher International Year Book 2004* (New York: Editor & Publisher Co., 2004)

a. Worldwide market as of January 2006, as reported by 2005 sales

daily newspapers for more than two centuries. Nonetheless, the daily newspaper that attracts readers with its content and, in turn, attracts advertisers that want to reach those readers has proved to be a very hardy catalyst. Other famous followers are shown in table 9-1.

The Catalyst Age

Newspapers, even the most successful ones, eventually found themselves clashing with other catalysts: radio and, later, television. Although they have shown they can coexist profitably, they are still competing to create a dynamic community of advertisers on one side and readers, listeners, and viewers on the other. Radio, television, and newspapers represented a clash of catalysts that took a long time to develop. Newspapers, after all, had only competed with one another for the first few hundred years of their lives. It took Sotheby's and Christie's more than two hundred years before they felt competition from eBay.

These sorts of catalyst collisions, however, will happen more often in our age. Catalysts are forming with increased rapidity and clashing with each other as well as with older catalysts. Technological change has made conditions ripe for creating catalytic reactions among diverse communities around the globe. Reductions in communications costs, increases in computer capabilities, and Internet-related innovations have made it cheaper to harness the hidden forces that can weld disparate groups into a catalyst community. And these technological advances have made possible highly scalable virtual platforms in place of congestion-prone physical platforms.

Twenty-five years ago, fixed-line telephones were the main way people and businesses talked to each other. Calling was expensive. A ten-minute telephone conversation between London and Hong Kong would cost £12.37 in 1981 ($43.60 in 2005 U.S. dollars).[2] Many countries, from industrialized countries such as Italy to less developed ones such as China, had poor telephone systems. Today, mobile telephones are widely used in most parts of the world. Many of the world's poorest people have access to a mobile even if they don't own one. A ten-minute conversation between London and Hong Kong only costs £5 (or about $9 in 2005 U.S. dollars).[3]

This dramatic decline in communications costs has wide ramifications for facilitating interactions among businesses and people globally. A little picture helps one see the big one. The mobile phone itself has become a platform where consumers and businesses can meet and engage in transactions. The surprising growth of downloadable ringtones opened many eyes to this. In 2006, consumers spent more than $5.4 billion downloading ringtones, such as fifteen seconds of Green Day singing "American Idiot" (see figure 9-1).

Now mobile phones are a place where consumers can buy and play increasing amounts of music, videos, and games. These ubiquitous computing devices pose challenges to businesses from retailers such as Virgin Records to cable systems such as Kabel Deutschland.

FIGURE 9-1

Mobile music revenues worldwide by segment, 2006 and 2011

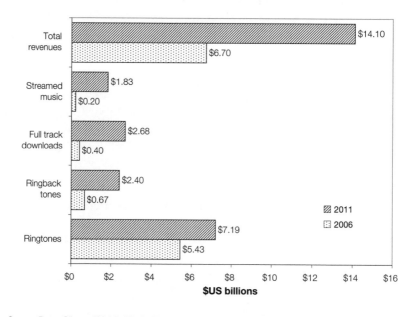

Source: Bruce Gibson, "Mobile Music: Ringtones, Full Track Downloads & Streaming, 2006–2011," Juniper Research, August 2006

The exponential improvements in computer processing and memory are well known. The power of software code to start and sustain catalytic reactions around computing devices is less celebrated. You can play "American Idiot" on your mobile phone because your phone has a software platform—probably the Symbian operating system—that helps software developers write the ringtone application and enables you to download and play your favorite songs.

Automobiles may be next (see the box "Catalysts Ignite New Markets: The Automotive Industry"). They have had computer chips and software for more than a decade. Now, companies are developing software platforms that can provide many services for the driver and passengers and can support applications that drivers could download themselves. Microsoft, for example, is working on developing software that provides *glanceable information* that doesn't require the driver to take her eyes off the road. A *heads-up*

Catalysts Ignite New Markets:
The Automotive Industry

It's Monday morning, and you're about to set off for a new-client meeting. As you slide behind the wheel and make your way onto the Autobahn, a translucent map appears on the windshield. The map, which was produced from directions you sent via Bluetooth from your BlackBerry phone to the car's GPS system, also calculates the distance and estimates the time of travel according to your speed. A few minutes later, a voice-activated alert warns you of traffic trouble ahead and reroutes you. Happily, it also tells you that you won't be late. Your in-dash iPod docking station allows you to calm your premeeting jitters with your favorite symphony. As you pull into the parking garage, your colleagues in Dallas call to tell you that they have updated your presentation and are sending you a new version to use in the meeting. Luckily, you opted for a car with mobile broadband connectivity; in less than two minutes, you are connected to the Internet via a docking station in the center console and are able to download the new version.

Sound implausible? Not if the automobile manufacturers have their way. They are making concerted efforts to blend transportation with content connectivity in order to revive sales and differentiate their products. And the catalysts behind this transformation are software platforms that are helping manufacturers adapt consumer entertainment and information technologies to in-car systems.

Getting all sides on board, however, means convincing manufacturers that consumers want these features and will buy cars (and pay more for them) with these innovations. The catalyst in this scenario—the software platform—will work to bring all sides together. It can help persuade developers to write applications, like maps and speech-enabled applications, and enable plug-and-play devices such as PCs and MP3 players that make it relatively efficient for manufacturers to offer these options. And one might argue that catalysts have already gotten customers on board; many of the applications that are being adapted for in-car use are those that consumers have already embraced and use regularly.

display would use the windshield to display maps and even caller IDs via mobile phone calls that come in while the driver is in the car.

Every device that has a computer chip has the potential of challenging existing catalysts or single-sided businesses. As we discussed in chapter 7, the contactless chip is a recent technological advance for payment cards that is leading to a collision among catalysts. In Japan, as we discussed, i-mode has installed contactless chips in its phones and has developed a payment system that rivals the existing card systems. It remains to be seen whether mobile operators elsewhere align themselves with the card systems, so that the mobile phone becomes just another way to pay with your MasterCard, or use this new technology to create alternative payment systems.

The tremendous declines in communications, computer processing, and computer storage costs were factors behind the expansion of the Internet. Our ability today to search the vast resources of the World Wide Web, however, is mainly the result of innovations—such as the uniform resource locator (URL) and the back and forward sequencing—that seem trivial in hindsight, like many of the most significant innovations in human history. And the World Wide Web is the main breeding ground for the new catalysts that are clashing with the old as well as each other.

Cracking the Catalyst Code

This book has described a framework that, used carefully, permits businesses to launch and sustain profitable catalysts. Much harder to describe is where the ideas for catalysts come from. What we have learned is that the identification of a good business idea with a two-sided platform is not enough to start, much less propel and sustain, a new business. Catalysts take time and patience. Some are discovered by accident; others emerge only after extended trial and error. Many succeed at creating a catalytic reaction and starting a vibrant multisided community only to discover that it cannot earn consistent profits over the long term. Some catalysts have to endure years of uncertainty and constant tweaking of design and pricing before suddenly taking off.

American Express started in the rough-and-tumble business of transporting things of value by rail, boat, stagecoach, and horse across the expanding frontiers of the United States in the mid-nineteenth century. Then, in a fit of inspiration, it developed the traveler's check, which transformed its business and ultimately turned it into a financial powerhouse.

Legend has it that the head of American Express, J. C. Fargo, took a vacation to Europe and found that despite his august stature in the United States, he spent a lot of time persuading banks to honor his letters of credit—the standard way that people traveling abroad in the late nineteenth century obtained local funds. When he returned, he instructed Marcellus Fleming Berry, one of his key employees, to develop something that could fix this problem for him and lesser tourists. Berry came up the idea of the traveler's check. It came in fixed denominations, was verified by having the purchaser sign when he bought the checks and again when he cashed them, and had exchange rates (they were fixed at that time) for major currencies in the middle of the face of the check so that unsuspecting travelers would get the right amounts of local currency.

It seemed like a perfect solution for a tourist. But for a business that wanted to issue the traveler's check, there remained a tremendous hurdle. American Express had to get banks and merchants—some thousands of miles away—to take the checks before it had any hope of getting consumers to buy them. It faced a classic chicken-and-egg problem of the sort that lies at the heart of all catalyst businesses.

Shrewdly, American Express didn't charge merchants or banks for reimbursing them for checks they cashed and even insured them against fraud. Armed with this attractive model, American Express aggressively signed on banks and merchants in Europe and the United States. After it got enough hotels and banks on board, it could make a plausible case to consumers. When American Express traveler's checks were first introduced in 1891, consumers bought less than $10,000 worth. A year later, they bought almost $500,000, and four years after that, nearly $2 million—serious money at the time.[4]

American Express had ignited a catalytic reaction between banks, merchants, and travelers—a very profitable one, too. Suppose your great-great-grandfather bought $100 in traveler's checks a month before his three-month trip to Paris. American Express earned interest on the unspent portion of the $100. Plus, it got to keep any amount that great-great-grandpa didn't spend—perhaps he had $10 left over that he kept for the next trip, which he never took.

This ingenuous product propelled American Express into a financial services and travel giant. Although traveler's checks are nearing the end of their useful market life, as cash machines and payment cards have become ubiquitous, American Express has remained the leader for this catalyst product for more than a hundred years. Even in 2005, American Express sold $19.7 billion of traveler's checks.[5]

Over the last few decades, other companies have reaped even larger revenues from businesses that have existed for only a fraction of the life of the traveler's check. Bill Gates's fortune, earned from a company started in the 1970s, is the largest in the world. Some believe he was just in the right place at the right time. He learned computer programming as a teenager, just before the microchip revolution made it an immensely valuable skill. He was enormously talented at writing efficient code and was a savvy negotiator to boot. Some suggest that his success was due to the fact that he was aggressive—and some say ruthless—in his determination to win. Most importantly, though, Bill Gates earned his place in history—and the great wealth that has funded his extraordinary philanthropic endeavors—because of insights into the business model necessary to marshal the forces of attraction between software developers, hardware makers, and users. He cracked the catalyst code.

Looking at Microsoft today—or Nintendo, or American Express, or Roppongi Hills—it is hard to see immediately that they exist only because an entrepreneur got two or more groups of customers together and harnessed the forces of attraction between them. Successful catalytic reactions seem so natural that outsiders don't think hard about the intricate effort, the delicate balancing, and the trials and errors that went into their creation and nurturing.

Stating the catalyst code is simple. Discover how to create value by bringing people or businesses together. Provide a safe and secure environment for this community. Help those who might be attracted to each other find each other and interact with each other.

Use prices and design to balance the interests of the various parts of the community.

What we have tried to illustrate in this book, however, is that implementing the catalyst code is complex—particularly in the novel settings where profit opportunities and risks are greatest. In our research on dozens of catalyst business, we took note of key traits and tasks that helped the most successful ones. The catalyst framework we have described here is not a cookbook for building a winning catalyst. Catalysts are too complex and diverse for that. Instead, the framework is a guide that entrepreneurs and investors can use to understand the special dynamics that underlie catalysts and the unique problems they invariably face.

We hope that the lessons in this book can help would-be catalysts and their investors ignite and sustain powerful reactions that will benefit society and give them a shot at building profitable and durable businesses. However, just as a trail map does not provide complete information to a climber who aspires to conquer a difficult mountain, general lessons are of only limited value to those who aspire to create another catalyst. Indeed, the most fundamental message of this book is that catalytic reactions are inherently hard to start and difficult to sustain and make profitable. Those who would succeed must find just the right balance that aligns the interests of the diverse members of the catalyst community.

Not simple in theory or in practice, but, like hitting a baseball, many have nonetheless done it—and some have done it very well.

Additional Readings

Baxter, William. "Bank Exchange of Transactional Paper: Legal and Economic Perspectives." *Journal of Law and Economics* 26, no. 3 (1983): 541–588.

Brandenburger, Adam, and Barry Nalebuff. *Co-Opetition: A Revolution Mindset that Combines Competition and Cooperation.* New York: Currency Doubleday, 1996.

Eisenmann, T. G. Parker, and M. van Alstyne. "Strategies for Two-Sided Markets." *Harvard Business Review,* October 2006.

Evans, David S. "The Antitrust Economics of Multi-Sided Platform Markets." *Yale Journal on Regulation* 20, no. 2 (2003): 325–381.

Evans, David S., and Richard Schmalensee. *Paying with Plastic: The Digital Revolution in Buying and Borrowing.* 2nd ed. Cambridge, MA: MIT Press, 2005.

Evans, David S., Andrei Hagiu, and Richard Schmalensee. *Invisible Engines: How Software Platforms Drive Innovation and Transform Industries.* Cambridge, MA: MIT Press, 2006.

Hagiu, Andrei, "Multi-sided Platforms: From Microfoundations to Design and Expansion Strategies." Harvard Business School Working Paper, November 2006.

Rochet, Jean-Charles, and Jean Tirole. "Defining Two-Sided Markets." *RAND Journal of Economics* (forthcoming).

Rochet, Jean-Charles, and Jean Tirole. "Platform Competition in Two-Sided Markets." *Journal of the European Economic Association* 1, no. 4 (2003): 990–1209.

Shapiro, Carl, and Hal R. Varian. *Information Rules: A Strategic Guide to the Network Economy.* Boston: Harvard Business School Press, 1999.

Notes

1. David S. Evans and Richard Schmalensee, *Paying with Plastic: The Digital Revolution in Buying and Borrowing,* 2nd ed. (Cambridge, MA: MIT Press, 2005).

2. Ibid.

3. General purpose cards only. See "U.S. Credit & Debit Cards Projected," *Nilson Report,* issue#865, September 2006; bank profit number is from Burney Simpson, "Bank Card Profitability," *Credit Card Management,* May 2005, 26–28.

4. Richard V. Heiman, "Worldwide Software 2004.2008 Forecast Summary," IDC report #31785, August 2004, Table 18.

5. Al Gillen & Dan Kusnetzky, "Worldwide Client and Server Operating Environments 2004.2008 Forecast: Microsoft Consolidates Its Grip," IDC report #32452, December 2004, Tables 1 and 2.

6. David S. Evans, Andrei Hagiu, and Richard Schmalensee, *Invisible Engines: How Software Platforms Drive Innovation and Transform Industries* (Cambridge, MA: MIT Press, 2006).

7. These are in the dollars of the time. The figures in this book are not adjusted for inflation unless noted.

8. Shipments for the fiscal year ended March 31, 2006. "Cumulative Production Shipments of Hardware / PlayStation®2," Sony Computer Entertainment Inc. website, http://www.scei.co.jp/corporate/data/bizdataps2_e.html.

9. Due to large R&D costs associated with the development of the PlayStation 3, the operating income of Sony's game division decreased to 8.7 billion yen ($75 million) for the fiscal year 2005 (ended March 31, 2006), down from 43.2

billion yen for the fiscal year of 2004. See Sony SEC filing Form 20-F (FY 2005), http://www.sec.gov/Archives/edgar/data/313838/000114554906001253 /k01183e20vf.htm#113.

10. Carl Shapiro and Hal R. Varian, *Information Rules: A Strategic Guide to the Network Economy* (Boston: Harvard Business School Press, 1999).

CHAPTER 2

1. Tom Jaffee, email to Terry Xie at Market Platform Dynamics, November 8, 2006.

2. "What is 8 Minute Dating?" 8minuteDating website, http://www .8minutedating.com/howItWorks.shtml.

3. Aristotle, *Politics* (328 BC). See Brent Dean Robbins, "Phenomenology, Psychology, Science & History: A Reading of Kuhn in Light of Heidegger as a Response to Hoeller's Critique of Giorgi," *Janus Head,* Vol.1, no.1 (Summer 1998), http://www.janushead.org/JHSummer98/BrentRobbins.cfm.

4. "Catch Of The Day A Tuna That Reels In $646,700," *South China Morning Post,* December 30, 2005.

5. The Tsukiji is a partnership of the government and private enterprise. The Tokyo Metropolitan Government owns and maintains the market. The Japanese Ministry of Agriculture, Forestry and Fisheries supervises the Tsukiji and other wholesale fish markets. Many different types of private firms make the marketplace work, including auction houses, stall owners, and dock agents. See Theodore C. Bestor, *Tsukiji: The Fish Market at the Center of the World* (Berkeley: University of California Press, 2004).

6. Of course, this isn't literally a free lunch. Trading consumes resources. The Tsukiji, for example, takes scarce Tokyo real estate; involves a significant number of employees to unload, sort, and distribute the fish; and requires auction houses to manage the process. The New York Stock Exchange, to take another example, incurred annual costs of $1 billion to support the $14 trillion of transactions that went through it in 2005. See "New York Exchange Annual Highlights 2005," NYSE Group, Inc website, http://www.nyse.com/pdfs/NYSE _AH_05_WEB_FINAL.pdf.

7. Guy Kawasaki, "Official Bio," About Guy page, http://www.guy kawasaki.com/about/index.shtml.

8. Bryan Glick, "7 Days—Chemdex Fell Through Lack Of User Support," *Computing,* March 1, 2001.

9. Exchanges are much more complex two-sided platforms than just matching buyers and sellers. See Bernhard Friess and Sean Greenaway, "Competition in EU Trading and Post-trading Service Markets," *Competition Policy International* 2, no. 1 (Spring 2006); and George Chacko and Eli Peter Strick, "The International Securities Exchange: New Ground in Options," Case 203063 (Boston: Harvard Business School, March 2003).

CHAPTER 3

1. Warren St. John, "Mr. Mover, Meet Ms. Shaker," *New York Times,* August 28, 2005.

2. "Traffic Rank for Youtube.com," Alexa.com website, http://www .alexa.com/data/details/traffic_details?&range=max&size=large&compare_sites =myspace.com&y=r&url=youtube.com#top.

3. Jessi Hempel and Paula Lehman, "The MySpace Generation," *Business-Week,* December 12, 2005, http://www.businessweek.com/magazine/content /05_50/b3963001.htm?chan=technology_ceo+guide+to+technology.

4. Rhys Blakely, "Google-eBay tie-up is 'biggest yet'," *Times Online,* August 29, 2006, http://technology.timesonline.co.uk/article/0,,20411-2332902,00 .html.

5. Number of stocks and bonds is from "London Stock Exchange: Trading Services", London Stock Exchange website, http://www.londonstock exchange.com/en-gb/about/cooverview/whatwedo/tradingservices.htm; number of transactions is from London Stock Group Plc Annual Report 2006, http: //www.londonstockexchange-ir.com/lse/finperformance/reports/results/ar06 /ar06.pdf.

6. Anick Jesdanun, "Myspace Plans New Restrictions For Youths," Associated Press, June 21, 2006, http://www.forbes.com/home/feeds/ap/2006/06 /21/ap2829384.html.

7. Wendy Davis, "Financial Services Companies Claim 28% Of September Web Ads," *Online Media Daily,* October 13, 2006, http://publications.mediapost .com/index.cfm?fuseaction=Articles.showArticleHomePage&art_aid=49547.

8. This term was coined by Adam Brandenburger and Barry Nalebuff in their book *Co-Opetition: A Revolution Mindset that Combines Competition and Cooperation* (New York: Currency Doubleday, 1996).

9. Estee Lauder Companies Inc. SEC filing Form 10-K (summary), for the fiscal year ended June 30, 2006, http://biz.yahoo.com/e/060825/el10-k.html.

10. "Cosmetics Queen Estee Lauder Dies," BBC News website, April 25, 2004, http://news.bbc.co.uk/1/hi/world/americas/3658375.stm.

11. "I-mode FAQ," *WestCyber Corporation,* 2000, as quoted in Tom Worthington, "Issues in the Wireless Internet," http://www.tomw.net.au/2001/wi.html.

12. NTT DoCoMo SEC filing Form 20-F, for the fiscal year ended March 31, 2006, http://www.nttdocomo.co.jp/english/corporate/investor_relations/referenc/form /pdf/200606.pdf.

13. Julia Angwin, Peter Grant and Nick Wingfield, "Hot-Button Topic: In Embracing Digital Recorders, Cable Companies Take Big Risk—Viewers Flock to the Devices, But Advertisers May Flee; Debating Ad-Skip Feature—Time Warner's 'Meteorite'," *Wall Street Journal,* April 26, 2004.

14. Pui-Wing Tam and Mylene Mangalindan, "Pets.com's Demise: Too Much Litter, Too Few Funds—Pet-Supply Site Sought Money But Couldn't Find Backers; 'It's Sad,' Says the Founder," *Wall Street Journal,* November 8, 2000.

15. Raymond Fisman, Sheena Ivengar, Emir Kamenica, and Itamar Simonson, "Searching for a Mate: Theory and Experimental Evidence" (research paper 1882, Stanford Graduate School of Business, Stanford, CA, January 31, 2005).

16. *Nilson Report,* various issues.

17. "Debit in the U.S.," *Nilson Report,* issue #833, May 2005.

18. "U.S. General Purpose Cards: 2004," *Nilson Report,* issue #828, February 2005; "Debit in the U.S.," *Nilson Report,* issue #833, May 2005.

19. Apple Inc. earnings and press releases, 2001-2006.

20. 2001 market cap data downloaded from Bloomberg, the data for NASDAQ and 2006 market cap data (as of August 23, 2006) downloaded from Yahoo! Finance.

21. Many companies now produce complementary products for the iPod—from better earphones than Apple supplies to home music systems that work with the music devices. However, Apple doesn't directly encourage these producers and doesn't provide them with any services. Therefore, these complementary products don't constitute a separate side and accordingly don't make Apple a two-sided business.

22. "PalmSource: Partners: Licensees," PalmSource website, http://www.palmsource.com/partners/licensee.html.

CHAPTER 4

1. This company is based on a start-up that we interviewed in the course of our research. We have masked details to prevent the disclosure of confidential information.

2. American Express Corp. 2004 Annual Report, http://www.online-proxy.com/amex/2005/nonvote/ar/AXP_annual04.pdf.

3. Sony charges $3–$9 per game on its PS2 platform. For a game that priced at $29.95 (e.g. "NHL 07" from Electronic Arts, as of October 2, 2006 on Amazon.com), the loyalty equals 10 to 30 percent of the price. Sony loyalty fee information is from: Adam M. Brandenburger, "Power Play (C): 3DO in 32-bit Video Games," Case 794-104 (Boston: Harvard Business School, 1995).

4. Steve McClellan, "Fox Breaks Prime-Time Pricing Record," *Adweek,* September 12, 2005, http://www.adweek.com/aw/search/article_display.jsp?vnu_content_id=1001096022.

5. "Christie's—How to Buy—Buyer's premium," Christie's website, http://www.christies.com/howtobuy/buyers_premium.asp.

6. "Crossroads Guitar Auction Realizes $7,438,624 at Christie's New York," Christie's press release, June 24, 2004, http://www.christies.com/press-center/pdf/06252004/guitars_062404.pdf.

7. "Symbian OS Phone Shipments Reach 14.4m in 2004," Symbian press release, May 10, 2005, http://www.symbian.com/news/pr/2005/pr20051857.html.

8. "Fast Facts," Symbian website, http://www.symbian.com/about/fast-facts/fastfacts.html; there are 6,778 software titles available for Symbian OS on Handago.com as of October 27, 2006.

9. "Microsoft Corp.: Windows 3.0 is here," Microsoft press release, May 22, 1990.

10. Lisa Picarille, "IBM Drags Feet on OS/2 Pitch, " *ComputerWorld,* April 17, 1995.

11. The practice of receiving "contingent commissions" from insurers led to lawsuits against some insurance brokers in the United States that in some cases did not disclose these commissions to the companies they were working for and manipulated the bids to the companies by the insurers. Several large brokers agreed to stop the practice and receive payment only from the companies they work for. See J. David Cummins and Neil A. Doherty, "The Economics of Insurance Intermediaries" (working paper, Wharton School, University of Pennsylvania, Philadelphia, PA, May 20, 2005).

12. There are exceptions, of course. When ATM networks were first started, if a customer of bank A took funds from an ATM operated by bank B, bank A paid bank B. As these networks matured and there was less systemwide benefit from having more ATMs installed, the networks changed their pricing models, and bank B paid bank A.

13. Michael Capozzi, "Insurance Marketplaces Among Dot Com Casualties," *Risk & Insurance,* June 1, 2001.

14. Craig Bicknell, "Death of a Digital Divide Bridge," *Wired News,* July 20, 2000, http://www.wired.com/news/business/1,37651-0.html.

15. Nick Wingfield, "Microsoft Scraps Slate Subscriptions, Offers Magazine For Free," *Dow Jones Business News,* February 12, 1999; George Anders, "Free for All—Eager to Boost Traffic, More Internet Firms Give Away Services," *Wall Street Journal,* Jul 28, 1999; David Carr, "Washington Post Company Buys Slate Magazine," *New York Times,* December 22, 2004.

16. "MobiTV Tops One Million Subscribers; Paying Users More than Double In the Last Six Months!" MobiTV press release, April 4, 2006, http://www.mobitv.com/press/press.php?i=press/release_040406_01.

CHAPTER 5

1. Jim Frederick, "TomorrowLand: Tycoon Minoru Mori Wants to Make Tokyo a More Livable City," *Time* (Asia Edition), August 4, 2003, http://www.time.com/time/asia/magazine/article/0,13673,501030811-472908,00.html.

2. Dan Jones, "RIM to Go Symbian?" *Unstrung,* September 5, 2006, http://www.unstrung.com/document.asp?doc_id=102926&print=true.

3. Rowena Vergara, "Rockford Joins Bigger Cities on Marketplace Craze Craigslist," *Rockford Register Star,* August 16, 2006, http://www.rrstar.com/apps/pbcs.dll/article?AID=/20060816/BUSINESS04/108160021/1017/BUSINESS04.

4. Alexis Swerdloff, "Bungalow 8 Owner Gives Yale a Class on Class," *Yale Herald,* October 24, 2003, http://www.yaleherald.com/article.php?Article =2537.

5. For more details, see David S. Evans and Karen L. Webster, "The Architecture of Product Offerings" (working paper, Market Platform Dynamics, Cambridge, MA, February 2006); and David S. Evans, Andrei Hagiu, and Richard Schmalensee, *Invisible Engines* (Cambridge, MA: MIT Press, 2006), ch. 11.

6. Malcolm Gladwell, "The Terrazzo Jungle: Fifty Years Ago, the Mall Was Born. America Would Never Be the Same," *New Yorker,* March 15, 2004.

7. Philip Brasor, "Leon For Men, Nikita For Women: Women Get Their Own Killer Matchmaking Magazine," *Japan Times,* October 10, 2004.

8. Ibid.

9. "Customer Service Home—Answer—How do I change or cancel my airline ticket?" Orbitz website, https://faq.orbitz.com/cgi-bin/orbitz_faq.cfg /php/enduser/std_adp.php?p_sid=LJKNfmji&topic=0&p_prodcode=&p_faqid =2425.

10. MasterCard data is from "MasterCard WorldWide: Corporate Overview," MasterCard website, http://www.mastercard.com/us/company/en/docs /Corporate%20Overview.pdf; Visa data is from "About Visa," Visa USA website, http://usa.visa.com/about_visa/about_visa_usa/index.html.

11. "Estimating the number of Linux users," The Linux Counter website, March 2005, http://counter.li.org/estimates.php; as of October 27, 2006, there are 10,460 software applications available for Linux on www.inuxsoft.cz.

12. Greg Gatlin, "Advertising, Not Sales, Drives Moves By Atlantic," *Boston Herald,* August 5, 2003; David Carr, "A Magazine's Radical Plan: Making a Profit," *New York Times,* August 4, 2003.

13. "Five-Year Ad-Revenue Summary: Monthly Magazines ($/000s)," *MIN Media Industry Newsletter,* January 2, 2006.

14. There were 75.7 billion transactions on general purpose cards worldwide in 2005. See "Global Cards—2005," *Nilson Report,* issue #853, March 2006.

15. "Electronic Money Usage Soaring," *Nikkei Weekly,* March 6, 2006; "Cashless Payments: Contactless Cuts Out Cash And Cards," *Electronic Payments International,* February 28, 2006.

CHAPTER 6

1. Dan Nystedt, "Microsoft Sees 15 Million Xbox 360 Sales by Mid-2007," *IDG News Service,* July 21, 2006, http://www.itworld.com/Tech/5051 /060721xbox/.

2. Microsoft Corporation SEC filing Form 10-K for the fiscal year ended June 30, 2006.

3. Dean Takahashi, "Opening the Xbox: Inside Microsoft's Plan to Unleash an Entertainment Revolution," (Roseville, CA: Prima Lifestyles, 2002).

4. "Microsoft Playing Out of the Box," *Hartford Courant,* November 4, 2001; "Game on! Sony, Nintendo and Microsoft Get Ready to Rumble in the Battle for North America's $8-Billion Video-Game Market," *Winnipeg Free Press,* November 10, 2001; "Game Wars," *Tampa Tribune,* November 19, 2001.

5. David S. Evans and Richard Schmalensee, *Paying with Plastic: The Digital Revolution in Buying and Borrowing,* 2nd ed. (Cambridge, MA: MIT Press, 2005).

6. Schelley Olhava, "The Console Plays: Worldwide Videogame Hardware Forecast, 2001.2006," IDC report # 28282, November 2002.

7. Based on the operating income (loss) data of Microsoft's Home and Entertainment Division results from Microsoft Corp. SEC filing Form 10-K, for the fiscal year ended June 30, 2006.

8. American Express was an obvious competitor as Diners Club expanded into the travel and entertainment industry, which was Amex's home turf and the source of its traveler's check profits. The American Express traveler's check program provided a payment device to the same basic communities served by Diners Club—merchants and consumers—and Amex already had expertise in getting both these sides on board. It was easy to see how a successful Diners Club card could eat into the traveler's check business. We know from the history of American Express that just as Western Union decided that it didn't want to get into the telephone business because it would cannibalize its telegraph business, American Express very nearly decided not to get into payment cards because doing so might cannibalize its traveler's check business. See Peter Z. Grossman, *American Express: The Unofficial History of the People Who Built the Great Financial Empire* (New York: Crown Publishers, 1987).

9. Schelley Olhava, "The Console Plays: Worldwide Videogame Hardware Forecast, 2001.2006," IDC Report #20282, November 2002; Schelley Olhava, "Worldwide Videogame Hardware Forecast, 2001.2006," IDC Report #26906, April 2002.

10. Todd Bishop, "Microsoft One Step Ahead with Xbox 360 in Stores," *Seattle Post-Intelligencer,* May 12, 2006.

11. Richard Digby-Junger, "Munsey's Magazine," *St. James Encyclopedia of Popular Culture,* http://www.findarticles.com/p/articles/mi_g1epc/is_tov/ai_2419100844.

CHAPTER 7

1. Byron Acohido, "Linux Took on Microsoft, and Won Big in Munich," *USA Today,* July 14, 2003, http://www.usatoday.com/money/industries/technology/2003-07-13-microsoft-linux-munich_x.htm.

2. "Season-to-Date Broadcast vs. Subscription TV Primetime Ratings: 2004-2005," TVB.org, http://www.tvb.org/rcentral/ViewerTrack/FullSeason/fs-b-c.asp?ms=2004-2005.asp.

3. "Craigslist Costs Newspapers," CNN.com, http://money.cnn.com/2004/12/28/technology/craigslist/.

4. There were 29,629 development projects under the GPL license as of November 9, 2006, according to freshmeat.net. See "Freshmeat.net: Statistics and Top 20," Freshmeat.net, http://freshmeat.net/stats/.

5. Russell J T Dyer, *MySQL in a Nutshell,* (Sebastopol, CA: O'Reilly Media, 2005).

6. Based on 2004 shares by shipments. Al Gillen, Mila Kantcheva, and Dan Kusnetzky, "Worldwide Client and Server Operating Environments 2005-2009 Forecast and Analysis: Modest Growth Ahead," IDC report #34599, December 2005.

7. Steve Hamm, "Linux, Inc.: Linus Torvalds Once Led a Ragtag Band of Software Geeks. Not Anymore. Here's an Inside Look at How the Unusual Linux Business Model Increasingly Threatens Microsoft," *Business Week,* January 31, 2005.

8. According to market capitalization data downloaded from Bloomberg.

9. "Key Traffic Statistics for NYTimes.com and Boston.com—April 2006 Report," New York Times Digital website, http://www.nytdigital.com/learn/pdf/NYTDApr06.pdf.

10. "Google Announces Fourth Quarter and Fiscal Year 2005 Results," Google Investor Relations website, http://investor.google.com/releases/2005Q4.html; NY Times Group's advertising revenue was $2.3 billion, see The New York Times Company SEC filing Form 10-K for the fiscal year ended December 25, 2005; Dow Jones and Co's advertising revenue was $0.96 billion, see Dow Jones & Company Inc SEC filing Form 10-K for the fiscal year ended December 31, 2005.

11. Alice LaPlante, "Google's Achilles' Heel," Information Week website, January 23, 2006, http://www.informationweek.com/news/showarticle.jhtml?articleid=177103024.

12. eBay Inc., SEC filing Form 10-K for the fiscal year ended December 31, 2005.

13. "eBay Analyst Day—Final," *Voxant FD (Fair Disclosure) Wire,* May 4, 2006.

14. Tony Waltham, "'Bot' networks on the rise, according to Symantec report," *Bangkok Post,* October 19, 2005.

15. Thomas Claburn, "EBay Makes Access to Its Web Services Free," InformationWeek website, http://informationweek.com/story/showArticle.jhtml?articleID=173602719.

16. "Walmart.com 2005 Sales Top $1 Billion," InternetRetailer.com, http://www.internetretailer.com/internet/marketing-conference/255804548-walmartcom-2005-sales-top-1-billion.html.

17. Frost and Sullivan, "World Banking (Financial & Loyalty), Smart Card Market, F268-33," 2004; *Nilson Report,* issue # 843, October 2005.

CHAPTER 8

1. Larry McShane, "Howard Stern Bids Farewell to His Fans, " Associated Press, December 16, 2006, http://www.breitbart.com/news/2005/12/16/D8EHB45O3.html; Andrew Wallenstein, "Howard Stern Redefines Video-On-Demand," *Hollywood Reporter,* November 28, 2005, http://www.msnbc.msn.com/id/10239045/from/RL.4/; Chris McGann, "Stern's Listeners Could Tip The Race, Some Analysts Say," *Seattle Post-Intelligencer Reporter,* August 7, 2004, http://seattlepi.nwsource.com/tv/185305_stern06.html.

2. Sirius Satellite Radio earnings releases, various issues, 2004–2006.

3. George Anders, "Free for All: Eager to Boost Traffic, More Internet Firms Give Away Services—No-Charge Policy Has Users Flocking to Egreetings; Will Revenue Follow?—'Spoiling' Another Industry," *Wall Street Journal,* July 28, 1999.

4. "Satellite Radio Option on Vehicles More Than Tripled Past Three Years," Autobytel Inc. press release, January 30, 2005, http://www.autobytel.com/content/home/help/pressroom/pressreleases/index.cfm/action/template/article_id_int/167; "Clear Channel Answering Satellite Radio With HD Rollout," *Business First of Columbus,* December 5, 2005, http://www.bizjournals.com/columbus/stories/2005/12/05/daily3.html?from_rss=1.

5. MasterCard had 25,000 while Visa had 21,000. See "MasterCard WorldWide: Corporate Overview," MasterCard website, http://www.mastercard.com/us/company/en/docs/Corporate%20Overview.pdf; "About Visa," Visa USA website, http://usa.visa.com/about_visa/about_visa_usa/index.html.

6. Tom Jaffee, email to Terry Xie at Market Platform Dynamics, November 8, 2006.

7. As of June 1996, Japan had 12.6 million mobile phone subscribers, while DoCoMo had 5 million in April 1996. See: "What On Earth? A Weekly Look at Trends, People and Events Around the World," *Washington Post,* January 25, 1997; "NTT DoCoMo Subscribers Top 50 Million," NTT DoCoMo press release, November 10, 2005, http://www.nttdocomo.com/pr/2005/000699.html.

8. "Octopus—Business—Statistics," Octopus website, http://www.octopuscards.com/corporate/why/statistics/en/index.jsp; "About Us," Octopus Cards website, http://www.octopuscards.com/consumer/general/global/en/aboutus.jsp.

9. "Octopus—Consumers—AAVS," Octopus website, http://www.octopuscards.com/consumer/payment/reload/en/aavs.jsp.

10. *Nilson Report,* various issues.

11. "TiVo Announces Second Quarter Results," TiVo press release, August 30, 2006; there are 113,343 thousand households in the U.S. according to US

Census Bureau, 2005 March CPS, http://www.census.gov/population/socdemo /hh-fam/cps2005/tabH1-all.csv.

CHAPTER 9

1. "Market News: Cut-Throat Christie's and Hirst in Mexico," The Telegraph newspaper online, March 14, 2006, http://www.telegraph.co.uk/arts /main.jhtml?xml=/arts/2006/03/14/bamarket14.xml.

2. Ellen Parton, email to Laura Gee at the economic consulting firm, LECG, March 28, 2006.

3. Based on UK mobile operator 3's calling abroad on Pay monthly pricing, posted on 3 UK's website, http://www.three.co.uk/explore/coverage/abroad PayMonthly.omp?plan=paymon&cid=31486.

4. Peter Z. Grossman, *American Express: The Unofficial History of the People Who Built the Great Financial Empire* (New York: Crown Publishers, 1987), 94.

5. American Express Corp. SEC filing form 10-K for the fiscal year ended December 31, 2005.

Index

About the Authors

David S. Evans and **Richard Schmalensee** have done pioneering research into the new economics of two-sided businesses and have contributed widely to the academic and business literature on the topic. The long-time collaborators together have written *Invisible Engines: How Software Platforms Drive Innovation and Transform Industries* and *Paying with Plastic: The Digital Revolution in Buying and Borrowing*, which has been called the "definitive book" on the subject.

David is a professor at University College London and lecturer at the University of Chicago and author of more than eighty academic articles. He is the Founder of Market Platform Dynamics, a strategic consulting firm that helps catalysts develop profitable product, customer, and business strategies. In his consulting work he has helped some of the world's leading incumbent and challenger catalysts devise strategies for long-term growth and profitability. He regularly consults with executive boards and senior management of companies across the digital media, high-technology, mobile, financial services, and software industries to help them capitalize on the opportunities presented by changing industry, market, and technology circumstances. He is an advisor to numerous new catalyst ventures around the world.

Evans has Ph.D. and undergraduate degrees in economics from the University of Chicago.

Dick is the John C Head III Dean of the Sloan School of Management at the Massachusetts Institute of Technology (MIT), where he is also a professor of management and economics. A former member of the President's Council of Economic Advisers, Dick is one of the world's leading scholars on the economics of industrial organization and its application to government policy and business strategy. The author of or coauthor of eleven books and more than 100 academic articles, he has done seminal work on the economics of advertising, pricing, and product bundling as well as two-sided business strategies. Dick is the Chairman of Market Platform Dynamics and serves on several other boards. He advises catalysts worldwide on strategic issues.

Schmalensee has Ph.D. and undergraduate degrees in economics from MIT.